LEAPING IN FAITH:
WHAT GOD DID THROUGH ELISHA
WHAT GOD CAN DO THROUGH YOU

Nancy Eichman

Leaping in Faith
ISBN: 978-0-89098-432-1

©2023 by 21st Century Christian
Nashville, TN 37215

All rights reserved.

Cover design by Brent Bruce

TABLE OF CONTENTS

DEDICATION

To Isaac, Titus, Ezra, and Silas, my precious grandsons

May you each grow up to be a "man of God" like Elisha.

Thanks to my family
Phil Eichman, John Eichman,
Phil, Amy, Isaac, Titus, and Ezra White

You jumpstart my faith and keep me hopping.

APPRECIATION

Deep appreciation goes to all the inspiring women whose examples grace the "A Leap of Faith" sections.

"As each has received a gift, use it to serve one another, as good stewards of God's varied grace: whoever speaks, as one who speaks oracles of God; whoever serves, as one who serves by the strength that God supplies— in order that in everything God may be glorified through Jesus Christ. To him belong glory and dominion forever and ever. Amen."
1 Peter 4:10-11, ESV

LEAPED OVER
ANY WALLS LATELY?

"...And by my God I can leap over a wall" (Psalm 18:29).

I don't know how many walls you have leaped over lately, but sometimes it's a stretch for me to get out of bed in the morning. The energy and coordination it takes to leap over a wall is out of my league. I think I'll pass on the wall leaping.

Fortunately, when David wrote such words of victorious faith in Psalm 18:29, he added a power-packed, qualifying phrase: "by my God." This meant that he was able to accomplish what seemed insurmountable by God's help. David proved this statement true when he killed the giant Goliath who was mocking God and His army. He also overcame the temptation to kill his enemy and God's anointed king, Saul. David's faith grew exponentially when he trusted God to eventually give him the kingdom He promised. David overcame spiritual challenges as well as physical ones through God's grace and strength.

David's words of triumphant confidence remind me of another hero of faith—the prophet Elisha. This powerhouse of faith shone as an example of light in a land of spiritual darkness, the kingdom of Israel. Elisha became adept at overcoming obstacles that were in his way. Whether providing more than enough food for the hungry, prevailing over a group of enemy soldiers, or bringing a dead son back to life, this man of God vividly demonstrated that God was in control and that He cared for His people. Some of them learned from Elisha's example so that they, too, could take leaps of faith and conquer the hurdles in their lives.

We can learn the same lessons. Elisha lived in times similar to ours today.

He was also surrounded by an idol-infested, evil-saturated society. Like our modern world, godly people were in the minority. Righteousness and integrity were rare. But Elisha's outreach to show God's power in a wicked environment touched both believers and unbelievers alike. Elisha made leaping over a wall in faith look easier.

Let's take a closer look at his life and see how he did it. We'll discover how we too can take a leap in faith. Taking his lead, we won't be performing the mighty works that he performed, but we can make an extraordinary difference in our culture like he did with the Lord's help. We will discover that with God, leaping over walls is not so impossible after all.

GETTING THE MOST OUT OF YOUR STUDY

To get the most out of your study, first read the Scriptures at the beginning of each chapter to get the context. Then, after you read the chapter in the book, use the review questions in "Going Further" at the end of each chapter to test your understanding of that chapter. Let "Who Else?" challenge you to find a biblical character who did something similar to someone in the lesson. See if you can figure out "who else" before you check the Scripture given. Can you think of other examples? In "A Leap in Faith," find inspiration to use your unique talents from contemporary women who have found their own ways to serve God. Check out "Jumpstarting Your Study" at the end of Chapter 13, which includes suggestions to further enrich your Bible class or personal study.

OFFERING A WILLING HEART

1 Kings 17—19

The workday probably began like any other ordinary day for Elisha. He fastened the yoke of oxen in front of his plow and began the grueling, mundane task of plowing the earth. His daily objective was the same—keeping the plow row straight while the backsides of oxen stared back at him. Not everyone was willing to do this day after day, but such uninspiring scenery gave him lots of time to think as he plowed.

No doubt Elisha felt blessed to plow in the rich meadowland along the Jordan River near his hometown of Abel Meholah (1 Kings 19:16). Yet even with fertile land, a farmer's crops in those days were subject to unpredictable damage from nature. After all his hard work, the farmer had few defenses against drought, pests, hail, mildew, erosion, and winds, which threatened his harvest.

If the 12 yoke of oxen (24 total) in the field that Elisha was plowing belonged to his father, Shaphat, the young farmer must have been from an affluent family (1 Kings 19:19). But even if they were prosperous, only the extremely rich who could hire others to work for them were exempt from the sweat and toil of field labor. Almost every able-bodied man, woman, and child was expected to work in the field from sunrise to sunset.

THE REAL GOD OF RAIN AND STORM

Elisha was fortunate to be able to plow the land at all. A two and a half-year drought had parched the land of Israel, but the drought had ended. It had been prophesied years before when the fiery prophet Elijah had bravely faced King Ahab with a grim weather forecast: No rain or dew was to fall on the land until God gave the word (1 Kings 17:1). That had been disastrous news for the nation's people. The drought turned the land into an arid ruin. Such an eye-opening sign was the Lord's judgment for Israel's disobedience.

Elisha and other believers of the true God knew that Ahab had led Israel away from the Lord to worship Baal. Ahab married Jezebel, the daughter of Ethbaal (meaning "with Baal"), the Sidonian King (1 Kings 16:31).[1] As a Phoenician princess, Jezebel instituted the worship of Baal as the state religion of Israel, imported her own prophets of Baal, and killed the prophets of God with Ahab's wholehearted approval (1 Kings 18:4, 19).

The purpose of the divinely ordained drought foretold by Elijah was ultimately to challenge Baal. In Canaanite religions, Baal was thought to be the god of rain and storm who controlled fertility in crops. When rain was withheld, it meant that Baal was periodically absent, submitting to Mot, the death god. When rain returned, Baal was revived to water the earth again.[2]

For many in Israel, the worship of Baal was thought to impact the crop cycle, but the false god's influence did not end there. Baal worship rites not only included human sacrifice to appease the god but also fertility rites, with worshippers performing sexual acts to prompt the god to make the people, land, and animals fertile (Jeremiah 19:5; Amos 2:7-8). So-called "holy" men and women staffed the shrines and served as prostitutes in Baal's temples.

To combat this degeneracy, God demonstrated his power over Baal in rain, storm, life, and death through Elijah in extraordinary ways.

THE ULTIMATE BAAL TEST

As Elisha plowed the rows of dirt, he might have thought back to Elijah's previous face-to-face confrontation with the prophets of Baal on Mount Carmel (1 Kings 18:17-40). Crowds from all over Israel came to see the dynamic spectacle. Some could not decide which god they should worship. Others were unwilling to make the commitment to serve the true God. Elijah announced the rules of sacrificing the two bulls and called for a decision.

From morning until evening, Baal's prophets danced and pleaded to their storm god with no results. They wondered why their god wasn't answering with lightning. Then they slashed themselves with swords and spears in the hopes that their out-pouring of blood would bring a downpouring of fire. After such fervor for Baal with no response, it was time for Elijah's sacrifice.

The prophet prayed to the Lord and called down fire on his thoroughly doused sacrifice. In one dramatic moment, all of it was immediately consumed. With this extraordinary demonstration of power, the people proclaimed, "The Lord, He is God!" (1 Kings 18:39). They rushed to slaughter all the prophets of Baal in the Kasson Valley as the Law specified (Deuteronomy 13). Then, with the accepted sacrifice and Elijah's prayer, God sent the much-needed rain.

Elisha, along with those faithful to God all over Israel, no doubt praised God for the victory of the Lord over Baal. Could they also have heard of Elijah's 14-mile run, propelled by God, to Jezreel ahead of Ahab? But the spiritual triumph was short-lived when Elijah received a message from Jezebel with a vow to kill him within 24 hours. Suddenly fear gripped the once courageous prophet, and he ran for his life. Elijah left his servant in the southernmost Judean town of Beersheba and headed off into the desert (1 Kings 19:1-3).

Then it was as if the prophet went missing in action. Where was the champion of those who believed in the Lord God? Why did he take off when his presence was desperately needed to stand up against Ahab and Jezebel? These questions remained in the minds of God's people. As Elisha plowed the field, he might have wondered, *What happened to Elijah?*

NO LOOKING BACK

As he might have been lost in his own thoughts, Elisha suddenly felt something around his shoulders. He stopped and saw Elijah the prophet himself! Throwing his cloak on Elisha symbolized that Elijah was choosing him to be his successor. God had called Elisha to follow in Elijah's footsteps as prophet.

Seeing Elijah move on, Elisha left his oxen and ran after him, asking him to allow him to kiss his parents good-bye. When Elijah replied to Elisha, "What have I done to you?" it was like the prophet was telling Elisha that God had chosen him, but the decision to leave his family would be his own (1 Kings 19:20). Elisha prepared a feast for them to celebrate his new role. They must have realized what an honor and challenge being God's prophet would be.

Elisha took a leap of faith in following Elijah. The young man was not choosing an easy life, full of prestige and glory. The life of a prophet could be difficult. Prophets were unpopular at times because they pronounced judgment, but they also offered mercy. They performed miracles, ministered to the people, and prophesied about future events. Though some in Israel hated the prophets, others respected them because they spoke words from God. Some kings even sought their counsel. Other kings persecuted and killed them because these messengers of the Lord spoke truth that monarchs didn't always want to hear. Prophets often walked a thin line between honor and death.

Elisha demonstrated his commitment to the assignment ahead. He slaughtered his yoke of oxen and burned the plowing equipment. He literally burned his bridges behind him as he looked forward to following Elijah and becoming his attendant. Although his future was unknown, Elisha was in good hands because he was in God's hands.

THE MYSTERY OF THE MISSING PROPHET

As they traveled over the land of Israel together, Elijah probably "filled in the blanks" and shared with Elisha what had happened to him after he ran from Jezreel and "disappeared." After Elijah traveled south as far as he could get from Jezebel to Beersheba in Judah, he trekked further and asked God in desperation to take his life (1 Kings 19). He was suffering from exhaustion, burnout, and depression. He might have wondered if the victory on Mount Carmel had made any lasting impression on the people to change their allegiance to the true God.

Twice, God provided an angel who gave him food and encouraged him to rest. Strengthened by the food, he seemed to travel in a roundabout route 40 days and 40 nights to Mount Horeb (or Mount Sinai), where years before Moses had received the Law. He spent the night in a cave, much like Moses did when God appeared to him (Exodus 33:22). Similar to Moses and the burning bush, Elijah had a personal encounter with God. This time, the Lord was not in the wind, earthquake, or fire, but rather in a gentle whisper. Elijah recognized the presence of the Lord and humbled himself by wrapping his face in his cloak. The prophet vented his feelings to the Lord, telling Him how he was the only one left serving Him. Elijah felt alone in his mission.

The Lord listened to his complaint and let him know that he was not alone. Seven thousand in Israel believed in the true God and had not worshipped Baal. This assured Elijah that his work had not been in vain, but had indeed been fruitful. In fact, even though Elijah's dramatic showdown on Mount Carmel was an awesome demonstration of God's power, the prophet's everyday ministry throughout the years had made a difference (2 Chronicles 21:12-15).

To make His assurance more personal, God told him that there was someone ready to be his disciple. This successor would continue Elijah's work so it would carry on after his death. He would be one of three people to bring justice to Israel: Hazel, Jehu, and Elisha. God told Elijah to go and anoint them.

Elijah's triumph at Mount Carmel was not a solo victory. Many in Israel still believed that the Lord was God. One important one was Elisha whom God had chosen to be Elijah's attendant. Elijah would not have to feel alone anymore. In Elisha, he would not only find companionship, but also a willing heart.

CALLING ALL WILLING WOMEN

We might not have been called in quite the same way as Elisha, but we all have been called by God. When He called us to eternal life, He also called us with a holy calling according to His purpose (1 Timothy 6:12; 2 Timothy 1:9). We are called to fulfill our specific reason for living. We each have a divine mission, chosen for our unique personality, talents and interests. No one else is exactly like you or me. Like Esther, we have been born "for such a time as this" (Esther 4:14). Every one of us has a distinct purpose in God's eternal plan.

Whether we are 19 or 90, God can use us in that plan. It doesn't matter if we are working inside or outside the home, starting a family or our own business, returning to school or retiring. He has been preparing in advance for us to accomplish what He wills us to do (Ephesians 2:10). Just like Elisha, we can be ready and willing to take on God's challenge for our lives.

HERE AM I, BUT SEND HER

Elisha's enthusiasm to follow Elijah and answer God's call is refreshing in our noncommittal modern world. He ran to volunteer. When a call for volunteers goes out today, which way do we run? Do we run to volunteer or do we run to the nearest restroom to escape?

Have you ever felt like you were so inadequate, fearful, or inexperienced that you felt unable to serve God when you had the opportunity? If you are sometimes reluctant, you are in good company. Some Old Testament servants of the Lord faced personal obstacles that made them initially less-than-willing to offer themselves. Moses was resistant. Gideon was afraid. Jeremiah felt unworthy. But the Lord changed their minds and used them in mighty ways.

God is faithful and provides for those He calls. These men had their faults, but they ultimately answered God's call to serve where they were. They discovered that God would offer His presence, protection, and power in whatever challenges they faced. We can experience the same thing. Like them, we can learn that God takes us where we are with what we have and uses it for His glory.

We might feel that God cannot use us because of our limitations. We might think that we are too young, too old, or too broken to answer "yes" to God's call. But He is greater than any of our weaknesses or obstacles. We can learn to depend on His strength instead of our own.

He might take us out of our comfort zone. He might ask us to try something we have never attempted before. If He wills us to do something, He will provide the way for us to do it. God will enable us to fulfill the mission He has for our lives. He "is able to do far more abundantly beyond all that we ask or think, according to the power that works within us" (Ephesians 3:20).

DISCOVERING YOUR PURPOSE

When Elisha found his mission as God's prophet, he gave a farewell feast for his family and friends. The feast also could have served as an occasion to mark the finding of his purpose. Although you might not celebrate with such hoopla, discovering your purpose is worth celebrating. Knowing what you can do for God is transforming. When you know what to do, you can devote yourself fully to it.

If you are searching to find how you can best serve in God's kingdom, first ask yourself some questions and reflect on your answers.

What do I love to do? What do I hate to do?

What gives me energy? What drains the life out of me?

What do I want to mold and leave better than I found it?

What group(s) of people am I drawn to help?

Where has God placed me "for such a time as this"?

Answers to these questions will help you know what specific cause or passion stirs your soul. This is crucial in understanding where you can best serve the Lord—your purpose. So how do you find your purpose?

Try out different tasks for God to see what fits. In your lifetime, there might be many spots you can fill. Pray for wisdom, ask family and friends to help you know your strengths and weaknesses, and take advantage of opportunities that come your way. They don't have to be dramatic adventures. These opportunities can be simple acts of service. You never know how God will bless your efforts, but you can know for sure that your labor will not be in vain (1 Corinthians 15:58).

As we go through different seasons in our lives, our possibilities to serve God change. The Lord knows our limits. He doesn't expect more than we have to give, whether it is our physical, financial, or spiritual resources (2 Corinthians 8:12). However, if God has blessed us with abilities, health, and opportunity, we have the privilege of offering ourselves willingly as our Lord did (Romans 12:1-2). When Jesus gave us so much, how can we give any less?

GOING FURTHER

1. Why is it important to understand Elijah's ministry to fully understand Elisha's mission? How did their ministries overlap?
2. How did Ahab and Jezebel lead Israel away from God to worship Baal? What rites of Baal worship made it so degenerate?
3. How did God demonstrate His power over Baal at Mount Carmel?
4. How did Elijah's prayer to God contrast with the prophets' calls to Baal? How does Elijah show us the power of prayer throughout his life (James 5:17-18)?
5. Why do you think Elijah felt depressed and alone and how did God provide for his needs? How can God provide for us when we feel depressed and alone?
6. What were some of a prophet's duties? How did Elisha demonstrate his willingness to answer God's call, while showing respect for his home and family?
7. How was Isaiah's willing heart response similar to Elisha's (Isaiah 6:8)? How can we develop more of a servant's attitude to respond like they did?

8. Have you ever felt like Moses, Gideon, or Jeremiah when they responded to God's call? Has there been a time when God used you to glorify Him in spite of your limitations?

9. Why is discovering your specific purpose for serving God so important in living an abundant Christian life? What can help you in this process?

10. Where do you feel you should concentrate more—building up your strengths or improving your weaknesses?

WHO ELSE?

Who else left their occupation to answer God's call (Mark 1:16-20; 2:14)?

A LEAP OF FAITH: BEING AN ANSWER TO SOMEONE'S PRAYER

Do you ever dream of doing something big for God, with visions of making a significant difference in His kingdom? But how often does that dream fade away, covered in piles of laundry, school papers, and medical bills? How can changing your baby's diapers or caring for your aged parents change the world?

It's comforting to know that God honors your service to Him both in the African jungle and playground jungle gym. He counts your faith as righteousness, even in small, ordinary actions. He values your heartfelt willingness to clean toilets, sit beside a bedside, or say a kind word. To God, these are big things, too.

Don't give up on your big dreams. Just know that God can use whatever circumstance you are in to give Him glory. Often it is in the ordinary that God uses His people to become who He wants them to be. Think how God later used the shepherd David, the farmer Elisha, and the fisherman Peter. God uses the ordinary to make extraordinary things happen.

Take, for example, Dorothy, who took a leap of faith and offered a free Bible to anyone who came to her garage sale. Her neighbor, Jasmin, had just prayed to God that someone could help her with her spiritual questions. She accepted Dorothy's offers of a Bible and a Bible study. After weeks of studying with Dorothy, Jasmin was baptized by the preacher. She told him, "I am so glad I met Dorothy, or I would still be lost."

Dorothy's act was simple, but significant and life-changing for Jasmin. So serve the Lord however you can wherever you are. You never know if you might be the answer to someone's prayers (Ephesians 3:20).

FOLLOWING IN SOMEONE'S FOOTSTEPS

2 Kings 2:1-18

When God called Elisha, the farmer's life changed dramatically. His destiny took a new direction. The meaning of his name—"God saves"—took on a new significance.[1] From his mentor Elijah, Elisha learned what it meant to be a true prophet of God. He learned how God's power was manifested in extraordinary ways. He learned what it meant to follow in another's footsteps to serve the Lord.

WHO IS THE LORD—GOD OR BAAL?

What would it have been like to be in Elisha's sandals during the years he was mentored by the prophet Elijah? No doubt the older prophet shared how, in the earlier years of his ministry, God not only demonstrated His awesome power to Israel, but He also bolstered Elijah's own personal faith. The Lord showed Elijah His provision firsthand in several ways so that he and others would know that "The Lord is God," the meaning of Elijah's name.[2]

Elijah Fed by Ravens (I Kings 17:1-6)—After Elijah confronted Ahab and foretold the drought, the prophet might have wondered how he would survive Jezebel's henchmen or the drought. He soon found out. God told Elijah to hide in the Kerith Ravine, east of the Jordan, where he drank water from a brook. God directed the ravens to feed him bread and meat twice a day. Elijah obeyed and took a leap of faith, overcoming any aversion he might have had to being fed by these unclean animals. He learned that God is in charge, and he must trust His will. Elijah discovered personally that *the Lord is God over nature.*

Elijah Fed by a Widow (1 Kings 17:7-16) — The brook dried up, so God called Elijah to go to Zarephath, a Gentile city seven miles south of Sidon, Jezebel's hometown. When he arrived, he asked a woman for some water and bread. She replied that she was gathering sticks for a last meal for her son and herself before they die. Elijah told her not to fear, but prepare his meal first, predicting that her source of flour and oil would last until the drought was over. She obeyed, and the three of them were daily supplied with food in the heartland of Baal worship. Elijah saw daily that *the Lord is God in enemy territory.*

Elijah Raised the Widow's Son (1 Kings 17:17-24)—Some time later the widow's son stopped breathing. The widow accused Elijah of killing her son, based on the pagan superstition that some long-buried sin of hers would bring calamity.[3] Elijah prayed, and the Lord brought her son back to life. This life/death experience confirmed to her that Elijah was a man of God and that he spoke the truth. Elijah found beyond question that *the Lord is God of life and death.*

IT'S "SUPER PROPHET"!

Many people, including Elisha, might have considered Elijah a "Super Prophet." Maybe Elijah wasn't called to leap tall buildings at a single bound, but he performed many mighty works through the Almighty. Elijah was not afraid to courageously confront evil kings like Ahab, who instigated the murder of Naboth through Jezebel's scheme and then stole his vineyard (1 Kings 21). This prophet could predict the end of a drought and the death of a king (1 Kings 18:1; 2 Kings 1:3-4). He could even call down fire from heaven on 100 soldiers, who had no respect for God or His prophet (2 Kings 1:9-12).

Elijah seemed "larger than life." His miracles were dramatic and a sign of judgment to those in apostasy. Elijah's were mighty big sandals to fill. How would Elisha ever hope to follow in those footsteps?

It would be understandable for Elisha to shrink away from such a challenge. The younger Elisha might have even questioned if he even looked like a prophet. Elijah's rugged clothes contrasted sharply with his wealthy contemporaries and undoubtedly registered a protest against the upper classes (2 Kings 1:8). But Elisha, like Elijah, had faith and confidence in the power and person of God. This faith drew them closer together in a common mission and ministry, even when Elijah's mentoring of Elisha drew to its end.

A WHIRLWIND TRIP

Finally Elijah's momentous last day on earth had come. Elijah, Elisha, and the sons of the prophets knew that he would be taken from the earth. What thoughts might have swirled around in Elisha's head as he contemplated the loss of his example and friend? Elijah had been a remarkable prophet to the nation of Israel. How could Elisha take on such a spiritual role? To accomplish the works that his mentor had performed, he knew he would need an extraordinary measure of God's spirit.

So when Elijah asked Elisha what he could do for him before he left the earth, Elisha asked for a double portion of Elijah's spirit. Much like a firstborn son's double portion of inheritance, Elisha asked his spiritual father Elijah for the power to fulfill the calling he had received from God (Deuteronomy 21:17). Only God could grant such a request, and Elisha realized that he could only complete his mission with God's help.

As Elijah and Elisha walked from Gilgal, the older prophet asked Elisha to stay behind so that the prophet could walk on to Bethel, then Jericho, and finally to the Jordan. Maybe Elijah was testing Elisha's allegiance to him at the end of his life. Elisha refused to leave his master. When the company of the prophets asked Elisha if he knew his mentor was leaving, Elisha asked them not to discuss it.

Then as Elijah and Elisha were walking and talking, suddenly a fiery chariot and horses appeared and separated them. Elijah was taken up to heaven in a whirlwind. At the sight, Elisha cried out in reverence and elation at such a triumphal exit from this world, "My father, my father, the chariots of Israel and its horsemen!" (2 Kings 2:12). Though the military images symbolized God's spiritual presence, they also could have meant that Elijah was more to Israel than Israel's military might. Then Elijah disappeared, and Elisha tore his clothes in grief.

ELISHA CONTINUES ELIJAH'S WORK

Elisha picked up Elijah's cloak that had fallen as he ascended. Would it now work the mighty works of God for Elisha? The new successor struck the Jordan, and it divided just as it had before for Elijah. When 50 men of the company of prophets witnessed this repetition of Elijah's miracle, they realized that now the spirit of Elijah was resting on Elisha (2 Kings 2:15). They bowed to the ground before him, acknowledging him as Elijah's successor.

However, Elijah had disappeared before. They asked Elisha if they could send 50 able men to look for the older prophet. They still were uncertain as to what had happened to Elijah. It seems they needed closure at the end of this important prophet's ministry to be certain if he was living, dead, or taken up to heaven. After a three-day search without finding Elijah dead or alive, they could spiritually lay him to rest and could now follow in the their new leader's footsteps.

TWO MIGHTY (DIFFERENT) PROPHETS

With Elijah gone, the years of training that Elisha had received from Elijah would give way to practical ministry. Elisha's mission to bring God's people back to Him was interrelated with dynamic components of Elijah's previous ministry. Elisha's ministry paralleled Elijah's in several ways. For example, they both:

- parted the Jordan River
- multiplied food to feed the hungry
- raised a dead child
- called down judgment from heaven on the unbelieving
- foretold that water would save Israel
- trained the sons of the prophets
- served as God's appointed lead prophet in Israel.

However, even though their purpose was singular, their manner of fulfilling it was unique. Their ministries mirrored their distinctive lives. Elisha lived longer than Elijah, and his ministry was about twice as long as Elijah's. Even though Scripture records Elisha performing more miracles than Elijah, Elijah's miracles were more dramatic and well-known. Elijah often dealt directly with powerful monarchs. Elisha also dealt with kings, but his miracles were predominantly to heal or help common people with their individual needs. At times, Elijah seemed a man of moods, either at the height of euphoria or the depth of despondency. Elisha seemed to be more even-tempered and self-controlled.

The two prophets came from different backgrounds. Elijah came from Tishbe, a small town on the east side of the Jordan River in a poor area of Gilead near the desert. It is easy to see then how he might have preferred a more rustic, solitary life. In contrast, Elisha was from Abel Meholah, on the west side of the Jordan River. He seemed more at home in cities like Samaria, where he had a home, and even palaces, where he was in the company of kings.[4]

In the New Testament Elijah is mentioned 29 times and Elisha only once. Truly Elijah stands out as a distinguished figure, appearing with Moses and Jesus in the Transfiguration. Elisha seems to follow in Elijah's shadow throughout his life. Even after Elijah was taken up to heaven, Elisha was described by a soldier of Israel's army as the one "who used to pour water on the hands of Elijah" (2 Kings 3:11). This menial task performed by a servant doesn't seem to be a job description of God Almighty's prophet. Yet when Elisha traded in his plow for a towel, he served willingly as an attendant to Elijah. The younger prophet followed in Elijah's footsteps until eventually he made his own path.

CRAMMING OUR FEET INTO SOMEONE ELSE'S SHOES

So we wonder—did Elijah and Elisha each fulfill God's individual mission for them in spite of their differences? Looking at the lives of the two prophets shows that although they were different in some ways, they were both well-suited for the roles God gave them.

Who better than the fiery Elijah to deal with the ego-driven Ahab and his domineering wife, Jezebel? Elijah's bold temperament, impressive miraculous wonders, and dramatic competitive challenge on Mount Carmel came at a time when Israel was on the brink of total apostasy. In contrast, Elisha's compassionate miracles and concern for common people reminded Israel that God still loved all His children and cared about them. Israel needed both these prophets to get the nation's attention to bring it back to God.

Fortunately, God fashioned them—and each one of us—for unique roles in His service. The Lord handpicked the personal qualities we need so that we all can best accomplish the purpose He has for our lives. This takes into account our background, talents, personality, even the time and place of our birth—none of which is an accident. There are certain tasks that only we each can do best.

However, the problem comes when we start comparing ourselves with others, especially when we are asked to follow someone's footsteps we consider exceptional. Whether we are asked to follow a talented teacher, organizer, or chairwoman, we can be tempted to question how we will ever stack up to someone so efficient, spiritual, or talented. It is as if we were Cinderella's sisters, with each of us trying to cram a big foot into her tiny slipper. In reality, our feet will never fit. We shouldn't even try.

It is easy to look at another Christian sister and conclude if we only had her IQ, education, looks, family, or friends, we would be more fulfilled and effective in God's service. If we aren't careful, we can feel we missed out and came up short when God handed out blessings and gifts. We begin to look at others' strengths and compare them with our weaknesses. When we do that, we will certainly come up deficient.

If we allow this envy to fester in our lives, we can start to believe that God isn't truly good. After all, when we trash ourselves, we are putting down the One who made us. We may begin to doubt God. Can we trust Him to carry through on His promises? Does He care about us? Are we truly important to Him? Such negative thinking can cause us to feel inferior. Our service to God will be stunted by our own bitterness and resentment.

GIVING UP THE COMPARISON GAME

We must realize that we were not created to complain or compare, but to contribute. As author Elizabeth O'Connor observed, "Envy is a symptom of lack of appreciation of our own uniqueness and self-worth. Each of us has something to give that no one else has." [5] How can we give up the comparison game of envy with other women?

Bolster our God-confidence. We need to remember how much He loves us. Nothing we can do will cause Him to love us any more or any less. Spend time with God and His Word. Find specific Bible verses to lean on when we need confidence in Him. Replace negative self-talk with affirming statements like Isaiah 43:4-5: "Since you are precious in My sight, Since you are honored and I love you… Do not fear, for I am with you."

Realize how self-destructive envy is. Some unknown sage said, "Envy slays itself by its own arrows." If we let envy take root in our hearts, it can slowly consume us. Proverbs 14:30 puts it this way: "A tranquil heart gives life to the flesh, but envy makes the bones rot" (ESV).

Focus on doing our personal best. The Apostle Paul gives us the key to keeping the right perspective about ourselves (Galatians 6:4-5). If we try to do our best work, then we can have the satisfaction of giving our all. God will judge us according to what we are capable of doing, not evaluating us against what others can do. The bottom line is that we are responsible for our actions. If we put our time and energy into what we can do, then we won't need to be concerned about how we compare with others.

Appreciate what unique qualities we have to offer. We don't have to be someone else to be effective for God. We can be ourselves. Although we can learn from others' experience and even follow their examples at times, God created each of us to take our individual place in His kingdom. When we accept who we are and find our place, God can use our uniqueness. Then we will be the happiest and most fulfilled.

We don't have to cram our feet into someone else's ill-fitting shoes to follow in their footsteps. It's just a matter of finding the right fit for *our* feet. Then we will be on our way to making our own path and blazing our own trail for God.

GOING FURTHER

1. In what specific ways did God build up Elijah's faith in the earlier years of his ministry? How did these experiences prepare him for later challenges?

2. Why do you think multiple miracles occurred during the events surrounding the Exodus, Elijah's and Elisha's ministries, Christ's ministry, and the early days of the church?

3. How does the meaning of both prophets' names reflect their mission?

4. What were some similarities in Elijah's and Elisha's ministries? What were some differences?

5. How were Elijah and Elisha well-suited for their roles? Do you think one was more effective than the other and if so, why?

6. How can comparing ourselves with others lead to bitterness and resentment toward God? How can constantly making comparisons stunt our spiritual growth?

7. How is spending time with God and His Word crucial to bolstering our God-confidence? What Bible verses affirm your faith in difficult times?

8. How is envy so destructive to our hearts? How can it also affect our bodies?

9. What analogy does Paul use to demonstrate how important everyone is in God's kingdom (1 Corinthians 12:14-27)? What are some unique talents that you can use for God?

10. Why is it important to concentrate on doing our personal best in what we do for God and not focus on what others are doing? How does this play out daily?

WHO ELSE?

Who else was taken up to heaven by God without dying (Genesis 5:22-24)?

A LEAP OF FAITH: SAYING "YES" TO GOD

Years ago in Zambia, Africa, if a mother died during or after childbirth, it was common for grieving, desperate families to bury her live infant along with her. Such a gesture was considered more humane than for the baby to starve without its mother's milk. One man could no longer stand this practice. He jumped into the grave, rescued the crying infant, and took it to Kathi Merritt at the Namwianga Mission near Kalomo. As the HIV/AIDS epidemic killed many parents in Zambia, their orphaned children were also brought to the mission.

It is there that Meagan Hawley took a leap of faith and found her calling. Since 2010, she has served as medical advocate and teacher for the babies and toddlers in the Haven. She works alongside caregivers called "aunties" who feed, bathe, change, nurture, love, and pray for the precious children.

The Haven offers home-based orphan care, each with house parents and 15 little ones. The children stay there until they are roughly two years old.[6] If possible, then they are transitioned back to their families with later follow-up in their homes to be sure they are adjusting well. Meagan's goal is to reunite each child with its family even though her work takes her far from her own family in America.

Meagan said, "I went to the mission field because I wanted my days to be spent fully serving and loving and exhausting my resources... People who choose this type of lifestyle are just like you. They are giving God their 'yes,' in the little things. It's nothing special we are doing here; we're just saying, 'Yes,' and we have a God who works powerfully through people... Our callings all look different, but we all are needed." [7]

TAKING GOD SERIOUSLY

2 Kings 2:19-25

People often suffer because they don't take things seriously. Take, for example, the quality of drinking water. Whether we are in a Third World county or in a city of our own nation, paying attention to something as simple as drinking water is crucial. In fact, it can mean the difference between life and death.

The adverse health effects of unsafe water on people and the environment are as current as today's news. You have probably heard of the damage to people's health in towns with a contaminated water supply caused by illegal dumping, sewer overflows, and chemicals spills, but have you ever heard of unsafe water from an ancient curse?

JERICHO'S CURSED WATER SUPPLY

Jericho was suffering from a curse, and the men of the city called on Elisha to help. In the past its flowing springs and tropical climate had made Jericho a verdant oasis in the desert. For centuries it was called the "city of palm trees" (Deuteronomy 34:3). The citizens acknowledged that the town was well-situated, lying in the fertile Jordan valley, but the water had become bad and the land unproductive (2 Kings 2:19). To understand why, we need to go back several centuries to Joshua's march around Jericho and its subsequent fall.

Why was Jericho's water cursed? Because Jericho was the first city taken in the Israelite conquering of Canaan, it was devoted to the Lord as a firstfruits offering of the land. The city and everything in it, including all living things, were offered to the Lord as "devoted things" by destroying them. Only Rahab and her family were spared because she helped to hide the spies. Afterward, the water became bad because Hiel disregarded Joshua's curse.

What exactly was the curse? Joshua pronounced a curse on anyone who sought to rebuild Jericho. He would lose his firstborn son as he lay its foundations and lose his youngest son as he set up its gates (Joshua 6:26).

What was the purpose of the curse? Jericho's disobedient pagan citizens were destroyed along with the city itself. The broken ruins of Jericho would serve as a perpetual reminder of God's judgment on the wicked Canaanites and also of God's grace in giving the Israelites the land of Canaan.

Why was Jericho inhabited soon after this curse? The curse referred to the walls being rebuilt and fortified. It later existed as an unprotected, unwalled city. The tribe of Benjamin was assigned to live in Jericho (Joshua 18:21). Later, Eglon, the king of Moab, attacked and took possession of Jericho (Judges 3:12-13). Centuries later, King David's embarrassed men hid out in Jericho until their beards grew back (2 Samuel 10:4-5).

What happened when Hiel of Bethel later disregarded the curse? During the reign of Ahab and probably with the king's permission, Hiel fortified the city by laying its foundations and setting up its gates. In the process, he lost his firstborn son, Abiram, and his youngest son, Segub (1 Kings 16:34).

How was Jericho still affected by the curse? The water supply was unhealthy and the land unfruitful. It is possible that the women were barren or miscarrying. Though the cause of the bad water remains unknown, some researchers see a possible link between the curse and schistosomiasis (bilharziasis), a waterborne disease affecting fertility and child mortality. This disease is caused by a fluke, which lives part of its life in snails like those found at Jericho. Other scholars think that the spring water of Jericho might have been affected by radioactivity in the rock layers, polluting the water and causing sterility.[1] God could have used natural methods like those above or whatever way He chose to cause the problem.

How did God remove the curse? Elisha asked the men of the city to bring him a new container with salt in it. Since it was new, it would not have any impurities in it. Even though salt is fairly ordinary to us, it held extraordinary meaning to them. Salt was considered a symbol of purification, preservation, and grace. Elisha might have also used the salt in a ritual symbolizing God's covenant of faithfulness with His people (Leviticus 2:13; 2 Chronicles 13:5). The prophet threw the salt in the spring, acknowledging God as the healer in cleansing the water. Elisha also proclaimed that never again would the water bring death or make the land unproductive. By removing the judgment and providing wholesome water, God demonstrated that His grace was abundant to His people.

THE CURSE ON THE BULLIES FROM BETHEL

In Jericho, Elisha had removed a curse by God's power. When he next traveled to Bethel, he delivered a curse through God's power. To understand why, let's go back to the root of Israel's many problems: the worship of idols.

How did Bethel's past play a part in the curse? When Judah's King Solomon died, his son, Rehoboam, became king. When Rehoboam demanded heavier labor from his subjects than his father, the people from the 10 northern tribes rebelled against Rehoboam. They formed the Northern Kingdom of Israel, established under the leadership of their king, Jeroboam. Jeroboam set up two golden calves in towns at the far northern and southern borders of Israel: Dan and Bethel. His purpose was to prevent the people from returning to Jerusalem to worship in the temple and giving their allegiance to Rehoboam. He didn't stop there. He set up shrines on the high places, appointed priests from men who were not Levites, and instituted his own festival to substitute for those in the Law of Moses (1 Kings 12:26-33). Jeroboam led his people down the path to pagan idolatry just to keep their loyalty and maintain control over them.

What prompted the curse? With such a rebellious past, Bethel became a center of Israel's apostasy and pagan calf worship. It is no surprise that this city would produce, in such numbers, youths who came out to taunt Elisha. They might have even heard their parents mocking prophets in the same way. When these hostile youths saw Elisha walking along the road, they jeered at him, saying, "Go up, you baldhead; go up, you baldhead!" (2 Kings 2:23). Elisha called down a curse on them in the name of the Lord. God sent two she-bears from the woods, which mauled 42 of the youths.

Why would God do this to children? Hauntingly, earlier Bible versions in this context translate the term for "youths" as "little children" (2 Kings 2:23). The Hebrew expression is best translated "young men" or "young lads," referring to boys from 12-30 years old. Examples of this usage include Isaac at his sacrifice possibly in his early 20s (Genesis 22:12), Joseph at 17 (Genesis 37:2), and men in the army (1 Kings 20:14-15).2 Elisha was jeered by youths old enough to know what they were saying. Little children would not have joined together to insult Elisha with such malicious disrespect and biting sarcasm. This unruly gang of at least 42 young teens would constitute a mob.

Was Elisha just a grumpy old man? Elisha at this time was probably not more than 25 years old, so he was not elderly. He might have lived about 50 years after this event (2 Kings 13:14).[3] He was most likely near the beginning of his ministry, which lasted from about 850-800 B.C.

Was the prophet too sensitive about his baldness? The term *baldhead* was an expression of scorn in a culture where baldness was scarce. Scripture doesn't indicate whether Elisha was prematurely bald or not. In fact, some think he might not have been bald, since his head was probably covered with a headdress to protect from the hot Middle Eastern sun. Perhaps the youths were using the term not as an actual description of his physical appearance, but only with derision and reproach. Others believe he had a different hairstyle, with his hair was cropped short on top.4 In their culture, luxurious hair seemed to have been a sign of vigor and strength (think Samson and Absalom). Maybe in taunting Elisha, they were comparing him to Elijah, who possibly was a hairy man (2 Kings 1:8). The youths may have been expressing their disdain for God's prophet who, in their eyes, did not possess the same power as Elijah.

What did the youths mean by "Go up"? This was not a necessarily a reference to the uphill location of Bethel but possibly to the miraculous translation of Elijah to heaven. It was their disrespectful way of saying, "Take off! You go too. Get out of here." No doubt Elijah's ascension to glory was known in this area. The youths did not acknowledge nor believe such a miracle from God, so they ultimately reviled God.

Why did Elisha curse them? Elisha did not use profanity, nor did he revile the youths. He only pronounced God's judgment and left the final work of judgment to Him. The Lord intervened when His name, His word, and His cause were under attack. Elisha had just begun his ministry as God's prophet, and these youths needed to be dealt with swiftly and decisively.

Why did the punishment seem so extreme? Ravaging beasts were often seen as judgment from God. Such punishment was prophesied for any who rebelled against God (Leviticus 26:21-22). At this time, Syrian bears were found in hilly wooded regions, where they could live in forests and caves. These bears came out of the forests and cut up or tore apart the youths to get their attention. We are not told whether or not they died.

What was God's purpose? This was an extraordinary wake-up call to the citizens of Bethel and Israel itself. God was trying to bring His people back to Him through smaller judgments instead of the larger judgment in store for them if they did not repent. However, they refused to listen, and the Assyrians would complete God's judgment in 722 B.C. by taking Israel into captivity. Although God's covenant blessings would bless those who obeyed God, His covenant curses would befall those who disobeyed Him.

TAKING GOD SERIOUSLY TODAY

If there's one thing people discovered about God during the days of Elisha, it was that God did what He said He was going to do. He could change His mind if people repented and changed their life of sin. But God was faithful to his Word and upheld righteousness. If people took God seriously and obeyed Him, they were blessed. If they didn't take Him seriously at that time, they ran into all kinds of trouble. We can learn from their example.

So how can we take God seriously today?

Take the worship of God seriously. Has worship become a same-old-boring exercise, or do you feel uplifted, inspired, and ready to take on the world afterward? Be intentional, and start the night before. Put out clothes and breakfast, if possible, so there are no surprises. ("Mommy, I can't find a clean shirt! Who ate all my favorite cereal?) Put your Bibles and purse near the door. Arrive on time. Avoid distractions by sitting toward the front. Be proactive with small children to provide restroom breaks and something to occupy them.

Pray for focus. Concentrate on the words of the songs. Visualize what they are saying. Consider ways they relate to you. Close your eyes during prayers, and reflect on the words. During the Lord's Supper, read a Scripture or song to keep your mind on the Lord. Passages like Isaiah 53 or the Gospel accounts of Jesus' last days are good choices to read. During the sermon, take notes if it helps you to concentrate. Challenge yourself to see how many points you can take away from the sermon to use during the coming week.

Take God's name seriously. God's holy name reflects His authority, reputation, and character. Long ago, the Jews believed that God's name was so holy that it couldn't be written. Today just open a novel or watch a current movie, and it doesn't take long to realize that God's name is taken too lightly. You know times have changed when the acronym OMG has become a frequently used shortened byword for God's name.

Many women say, *I just wasn't thinking when those words spilled out.* To prevent "speak leak," think ahead. Put your brain in gear before revving up your mouth. Find your own inoffensive words in advance like "Ohhhh! That hurts! I can't believe it! Fantastic! Congratulations!" When an occasion comes when you might let something dishonorable to God slip from your lips, pick an appropriate alternative or say nothing. Jesus declared that on the Day of Judgment everyone will give an account for each careless word spoken (Matthew 12:36-37).

Take God's Word Seriously. No matter how knowledgeable you are of God's Word, there is always more to learn. The Scriptures can challenge you if you approach them with a fresh perspective. Try to use a different approach or a unusual focus to gain new insights that you might have missed before. Digging into Bible study aids like commentaries, concordances, study Bibles, and Bible dictionaries can help you mine new details. Don't forget free online resources. Archaeological handbooks and background commentaries bring Bible times to life. All these aids can help you walk in the sandals of Bible characters and see the world from their perspective.

Be a Bible detective, and search for clues in the details of the passage context. Watch for connections between people (how Rahab was related to Ruth), and note patterns in the text (repetition of phrases in the Psalms). Look for similarities and differences in people (contrasts in father David and son Solomon as kings of Judah). Read the text out loud in a different version in a different setting to "feel" what it was like (reading the Sermon on the Mount on a hillside). Use a grid or chart to make it easier to understand a difficult theological passage or complicated narrative.[5] Taking your Bible study seriously will bring exciting and rich rewards that will make you eager to delve deeper into the Word.

Take God's promises seriously. Evangelist D.L. Moody once said, "God never made a promise that was too good to be true." [6] Yet how often do you think about God's awesome promises like these?

- His abiding presence (Matthew 28:20),

- Forgiveness of sins (1 John 1:9),

- Escape from temptation (1 Corinthians 10:13),

- Answers to your prayers (1 John 5:14),

- Eternal life (1 John 2:25).

How do you know that He will keep His promises? He has never failed to honor a promise, and He is faithful (Hebrews 10:23). We just need to be faithful ourselves (Hebrews 10:36). The Apostle Peter wrote, "His divine power has granted to us everything pertaining to life and godliness, through the true knowledge of Him who called us by His own glory and excellence. For by these He has granted to us His precious and magnificent promises, so that by them you may become partakers of the divine nature," (2 Peter 1:3-4). Now those are marvelous blessings to take seriously!

GOING FURTHER

1. What was the curse that Joshua put on Jericho? In spite of the curse, how could Jericho be inhabited after the fall of Jericho?
2. Who disregarded the curse of Jericho? What were the consequences?
3. How was the curse still affecting the lives of Jericho's inhabitants? How did God through Elisha remove it?

4. What was Bethel's history as a center of idol worship in Israel? How might the bullies of Bethel have been influenced by this culture?

5. What was the stigma of baldness at that time? What else about the bullies' mockery made it so disrespectful to God and His prophet?

6. Why do you think Elisha pronounced God's judgment on the young men? What were the consequences for them?

7. How can you be intentional in preparing to worship God? What are some ways you can eliminate distractions and focus better in worship?

8. How has the name of God become unholy and commonplace in our society? What are some ways you can be proactive by thinking ahead before you speak?

9. What study aids do you think would help you most in your Bible study and why? What different approaches to Bible study can you utilize to make your study more enriching and applicable?

10. What are some of the promises of God that mean the most to you and why? How can you be confident that God will deliver on His promises?

WHO ELSE?

Who else was attacked by a wild animal (1 Kings 13:21-25)?

A LEAP OF FAITH: SEWING FOR THE MASTER

While watching a TV program about "Little Dresses for Africa," Ann Preston Maple was inspired to start a sewing ministry in her congregation. Taking a leap of faith, she asked if anyone was interested in joining her. Around 60 women came with their sewing machines and sergers. Everyone found something to do–cut, iron, sew, pack, or organize materials. Because of the huge interest, permanent space in the building was found for the project. With some church handymen to help, unused classrooms were renovated to provide space to work and store materials, like thread, fabric, ribbon, lace, buttons, and rickrack. These rooms were wired to provide enough outlets for the sewing machines.

The ladies publicized their need for supplies, and soon people from all over were offering materials and money for the project. They discovered that they were spending most of their time fixing old machines, so they held fundraisers to purchase inexpensive new ones. When their supplies ran low, the Lord provided. Once they drove to another state to pick up a van full of fabric.

Dresses have been sent to over 30 countries, including Nicaragua, where each summer the congregation sends a team who can personally deliver them. Sewing machines and sergers are sent there, and those interested are taught to sew. The ladies send shorts and T-shirts for the boys as well as diaper bags, blankets, bibs, and T-shirt diapers. Every item is sized and bagged, including a "we care" message. Some children have never previously owned a dress or shirt and shorts. Cathy Meadows, who sews with the program, is amazed at how excited the children are. Some are even proud of their plastic resealable bags! [7]

TRUSTING WHEN
IT DOESN'T MAKE SENSE

2 Kings 3

What if you were President of the United States and an enemy army suddenly threatened you? Whom would you trust? In whom would you put your faith? Would you call in your advisors? Would you rely on your allies? Would you pray to your God?

King Joram (also known as Jehoram) faced such a national crisis (2 Kings 3). Though Joram was not as evil as his father, Ahab, they both put more faith in idols than in God. In facing a similar situation years before, Ahab had consulted 400 prophets who told him what he wanted to hear. Ahab suffered military defeat and subsequent death from following these false prophets' untrustworthy counsel (1 Kings 22:1-40).

So Joram decided to trust in a military partnership with Jehoshaphat, king of Judah, who had more military experience than he did. Such an alliance should prove to be an advantage if an enemy attacked. That is exactly what their enemy Moab was ready to do.

KINGS MAKING FOOLISH DECISIONS

King Mesha of Moab foolishly decided to rebel against Israel. Moab had been under subjection to King David (2 Samuel 8:2). When Solomon's kingdom split, the domination over Moab shifted to the Northern Kingdom. Mesha had to raise sheep and supply Israel with 100,000 lambs and the wool of a 100,000 rams. He was getting tired of shouldering such a heavy burden.

Joram rallied Israel to fight Mesha and also called Jehoshaphat, king of Judah, to join him. Family ties proved powerful as these kings were related by marriage. Ahab had given his daughter,

Athaliah, to Jehoshaphat's son, Jehoram (a second Jehoram), in marriage (2 Kings 1:17; 2 Chronicles 18:1). Joram and Athaliah were siblings, children of Ahab, so Jehoshaphat's daughter-in-law was Joram's sister. Jehoshaphat agreed to help Joram, saying, "I will go up; I am as you are, my people as your people, my horses as your horses" (2 Kings 3:7).

Years before, Jehoshaphat had made a similar statement when he joined forces with Ahab to recapture Ramoth Gilead from the King of Aram (1 Kings 22:4). At that time, Ahab disguised himself to hide his identity while urging Jehoshaphat to don his royal robes in battle. The King of Aram commanded his captains to target Ahab alone, and they almost mistakenly killed Jehoshaphat instead because they thought he was Ahab. However, a random arrow hit Ahab and killed him anyway. It would seem that such a close encounter with death would prevent Jehoshaphat from being an ally with such a devious family again, but Jehoshaphat foolishly became entangled with Joram's conflict.

DESERT MARCH TO DISASTER?

So the armies set off, led by Joram and Jehoshaphat, along with the army of the king of Edom. They marched south and then east through the desert of Edom, a journey of about seven days. This trip around the Dead Sea put them at a military advantage to enter Moab from the south. They hoped that Moab would not be as heavily armed at that border as they probably were in the north.

However, it was a foolish and disastrous march for thirsty soldiers and their animals. The kings had likely planned to find water there, but they found none. In such a dry climate, dehydration came quickly, and men and beasts ultimately died of thirst. Joram considered this unexpected crisis a disaster brought on them from God.

As with Ahab before, Jehoshaphat asked Joram if a prophet was available to ask God for help. Unexpectedly, an officer of Joram mentioned that Elisha was there. The officer added that Elisha "used to pour water on the hands of Elijah," meaning that Elisha had been Elijah's personal servant (2 Kings 3:11). Elisha might have been sent there by the Lord or served as a kind of army chaplain who represented God's presence and made sacrifices. As a sign of respect, the leaders went to see Elisha.

DIGGING DESERT DITCHES

Elisha didn't flatter Joram, but sternly told him to seek counsel from the prophets of his parents. Joram countered that it was the Lord who called the kings together to hand them over to Moab. Elisha then confirmed that if the godly Jehoshaphat had not been there, the prophet would not have looked at or noticed him.

Then Elisha asked for a harpist. Some scholars think that the purpose of this soothing harp music was to promote calm after the angry exchange with Joram.[1] Others believe that prophets at this time used various ways to make them more receptive to oracles from God. Music played a part in inducing a trancelike, ecstatic state to receive divine messages, much like the procession of prophets in 1 Samuel 10:5. Imagine an ordinary harp "playing" such an integral part in prophecy.

While the harpist played, the Spirit of the Lord came upon Elisha. Elisha told the kings that the Lord commanded them to make the valley full of ditches (2 Kings 3:16). He predicted that the valley would be full of water from the Lord without wind or rain. This was quite a feat because typically in a desert, rain was the usual source of moisture (if there was any), and wind was a precursor to rain. The water would seem to come from nowhere. In providing water for the men and animals, God would also provide a way to triumph over Moab. God's power would take something ordinary that seemed impossible to them and make it easy, "a slight thing in the sight of the Lord" (2 Kings 3:18).

The soldiers dug the ditches, even though obeying the order might not have made sense to them. After all, who in their right mind would dig ditches for water in the desert? The next morning, about the time of the morning sacrifice, water was flowing from the higher elevations of Edom. The ditches were full of water. The soldiers and animals drank freely and were saved from death.

THE DEVASTATION OF MOAB

Meanwhile in the Moabite camp, the soldiers were stationed on the border. They woke up and saw something extraordinary: the red of the rising sun on the water in the ditches. Not expecting water in the desert, they assumed they saw blood from the three nations slaughtering one another. After all, had not Israel, Judah, and Edom been previously hostile to one another? The Moabites rose up to plunder the Israelite camp. What a shock to find three armies poised to meet them! Instead, the Israelites slaughtered the Moabites and invaded their land.

Following God's directions, the armies proceeded to ravage Moab's cities, cripple Moab's economy, and wipe out their agriculture by:

- overthrowing every fortified city and major town,

- cutting down every good tree,

- stopping up all the springs,

- ruining every good field with stones (2 Kings 3:19).

These severe measures were more stringent than the rules of war in the Law, but they were typical of invading armies punishing their enemies to speed up their surrender (Deuteronomy 20:19-20). God had a purpose in His commands to devastate the rebellious nation of Moab. Although springs and fields could eventually be cleared, completing the task could take years of exhaustive labor. Trees prevented erosion, and their loss would take away valuable fruit, shade, and firewood. Such actions would set Moab back for years in cleanup and restoration.

After all the destruction, only the city of Kir Hareseth was left standing. This capital of Moab was located on the brow of a rocky steep hill, surrounded by a narrow, deep valley and enclosed by high mountains on all sides. Such a strategic location made breaking through the walls difficult, even with Israelite slingers aiming at anyone visible on the wall. With 700 swordsmen, King Mesha made an effort to break through to the King of Edom, but Mesha's efforts failed.

In a last-ditch effort, Mesha sacrificed his firstborn son, the crown prince, on the wall of the city. The king offered him in the hopes that the Moabite god, Chemosh, would act to deliver them. This public display of placating a pagan deity on the wall of the city by sacrificing the crown prince was a rare and desperate act. In a war of several foolish decisions, Mesha's gruesome sacrifice of his son was the most foolish of all. It just didn't make sense.

For some reason, the Israelite coalition then withdrew and returned home because of an unexplained "great wrath against Israel" (2 Kings 3:27). It is uncertain why they dispersed at what seemed the moment of total victory. Did the desperate act of sacrifice stir the Moabites to fury and provoke them to storm the coalition and force their withdrawal? Did a superstitious belief that the appeased Moabite god, Chemosh, would turn on them in his home territory provoke the Israelites to go home?[2] Did the Israelites recoil in horror at such a cruel act to appease a pagan god and make them want to leave the scene? After fighting so hard, how could they leave content with only a near-victory in hand?

Questions still remain about the outcome. Israel's mission was fulfilled in that Moab was handed over to Israel (2 Kings 3:18). Moab's rebellion was suppressed, her power broken, and the nation was devastated. Though we don't know for sure what happened at the end of the conflict, we do know Moab remained a thorn in the side of Israel. Over 40 years later, when Jehoash reigned in Israel, Moabite bands of raiders invaded the country every spring (2 Kings 13:20). Because Israel didn't completely finish their mission, Moab remained independent and served as a menace to the nation of Israel for years to come.

BLINDFOLDED ON A ROLLER COASTER

If there had been a hidden camera when the shovels started swinging and digging those ditches in the desert, we probably would have heard some intriguing conversations:

"Why are we digging these ditches in the desert?"

"Don't they know we're about to die of thirst?"

"Which of those kings had this crazy idea?"

"Wasn't it the prophet Elisha who got the message from God?"

It was a wonder that the kings of Israel, Judah, and Edom didn't have a riot on their hands. Did the soldiers believe the words of Elisha? Or did they fear their leaders too much to disobey? Did some actually trust even when it didn't make sense?

Have you ever been in a similar situation? Somehow life is not making any sense, yet you are called to trust God despite the faith-shaking confusion, sorrow, or anger you are feeling. You might feel like you have been blindfolded on a roller coaster. At times like that, you have to hold on tight to God and feel confident that He will be right there with you for the ride.

HANGING ON

How do we hang on to God when we can't see our way? There are no easy answers, but we can delve a little deeper into the questions.

Why can't we always understand God's plan? Though we try, we will never comprehend how or why God works as He does. We just know that His ways are higher and deeper than we could ever make sense of this side of eternity. "For My thoughts are not your thoughts, nor are your ways My ways," declares the Lord" (Isaiah 55:8). We don't have to understand the details of God's plans to walk with Him. He just asks us to obey Him and ultimately trust Him whether it makes sense to us or not.

Why doesn't God always fit our perception of Him? God is much bigger than we can imagine. We can't put Him "in a box" of our own choosing. Because of our finite perspective, in our minds we limit what God can do. When we do that, we are walking by sight, not by faith. When circumstances don't make sense, we might think God should act a certain way that we can understand. But our God has all power. He knows everything. He is everywhere at once. He really doesn't fit into our ideas of what He should be. Solomon understood this well: "But will God indeed dwell on the earth? Behold, heaven and the highest heaven cannot contain You, how much less this house which I have built!" (1 Kings 8:27)

How can God work in all things for the good of His people (Romans 8:28)? How many times have we attempted to make sense of every circumstance and then set ourselves up for confusion and disappointment? In working this out, however, we might miss something important that God wants us to eventually recognize if we continue to trust Him. We don't have to fit together each piece of God's intricate puzzle of life. Joseph discovered this when he told his brothers, "You intended to harm me, but God intended it for good to accomplish what is now being done, the saving of many lives" (Genesis 50:20).

Why do we feel we have to run the universe? Sometimes our need to control our lives is like telling God, "You can't handle everything. We can take it from here. Thank You." But this attitude can backfire when the trials of life vividly show us how little control we have. We just can't handle all the details, but God can. We need to let God handle things and put our trust in Him. "Trust in the Lord with all your heart and do not lean on your own understanding. In all your ways acknowledge Him, and He will make your paths straight" (Proverbs 3:5-6).

Why is it sometimes so difficult to pray? Those times we find it hardest to pray are often the times we need to pray the most. When life doesn't make sense, we can learn how to pray like we have never prayed before. God already knows our confusion and pain, so we are not telling him anything He doesn't know. Instead we pray to entrust our lives to God in humility. "Seek the Lord and his strength; seek his presence continually!" (1 Chronicles 16:11, ESV)

Where do we turn to make sense of life? Troubling, senseless events prompt us to look to Jesus in a senselessly broken world. It doesn't make much sense for the Son of God to leave heaven to suffer and die on earth on a cross (Philippians 2:5-11). This paradox makes the incarnation so incredible. But when we understand that love compelled Him to offer us eternal life, His sacrifice gives our lives meaning and hope (John 15:13).

Why can't God be on our timetable? We want action, and we want it now! God is not confined by time, and He will act whenever He wills. Trusting Him in this takes the form of patience when we don't understand what life throws at us. "You too be patient; strengthen your hearts, for the coming of the Lord is near" (James 5:8). When the Lord takes us home to heaven, then we will understand.

GOING FURTHER

1. What foolish decisions did the kings of Israel, Judah, and Moab make? How were the soldiers and animals affected by their disastrous desert march?

2. What did the officer's description of Elisha mean (2 Kings 3:11)? How was Elisha's task similar to Jesus' during the Passover meal with His disciples?

3. Why do you think Elisha called for a harpist? What was its effect on him?

4. How did God save His people in two ways through the water He provided? Why do you think the Moabites thought the water was blood?

5. What did God command the troops to do to cripple Moab? What specific consequences did these severe measures have on Moab's economy?

6. Why do you think the coalition dispersed after Mesha sacrificed his son? How did Moab remain a menace to Israel years later?
7. When do God's plans sometimes not make sense to you? What does it mean when God says that His ways and thoughts are higher than ours?
8. How does looking to Jesus help us make sense of life? Even though He is the Son of God, how can we relate to Him in an important way?
9. Have you ever tried to make sense of circumstances and then been disappointed? What part does prayer play to help us trust God when life's circumstances go beyond our understanding?
10. Was there a time when you wanted God to work on your timetable, but later was glad that He didn't? What did you learn from your experience?

WHO ELSE?
Who else was aided by the playing of a harp (1 Samuel 16:23)?

A LEAP OF FAITH: SERVING ON THE ROAD AGAIN FOR GOD
Since Vickie Bass and her husband, Ed, have served Churches of Christ in such places as Kentucky, Wyoming, Hawaii, and New Zealand, they have had a heart for remote, small-town congregations. Many of these churches, especially in the less-populated western United States, have fewer than 30 members, and some are closing their doors. Once while rotating among several small churches and seeing the tremendous need for assistance, Vickie asked Ed, "Wouldn't it be great if we could do something like that full-time?" [3]

Now Vicki and Ed are doing just that, with no cost to the congregations they serve. With a leap of faith, they found a sponsoring congregation and began a ministry called the Barnabas Journey, after the "son of encouragement" in Acts. In fact, they see their main purpose as encouraging and listening.

Living in their RV, they spend about a month at each church to encourage the members and do whatever they need to help. They rotate between working in the southern states during the colder months and the northern states during the warmer months. Having spent most of her life in Wyoming, Vickie's varied background fits this nomadic life well. She knows how to snowmobile and hunt. She also served as cook for groups camping near Yellowstone National Park.

At each congregation, Ed may preach and teach, while Vickie may teach a ladies' or children's class and help with a ladies' retreat. They have assisted with Vacation Bible School, putting chairs together, and doing janitorial duties. Ed says that the churches' "response has been as much or more of an encouragement to us than any encouragement we have given them." [4]

CHAPTER 5

SEEING THE IMPORTANCE
OF LITTLE THINGS

2 Kings 4:1-7; 6:1-7

As God's prophet, Elisha was acquainted with the highest and lowest in society, from wealthy kings to poor servants. Elisha tapped into God's power to help them in their time of need. In every instance, God showed that He cared about them, whether it was about matters of international importance of the high and mighty or the smallest detail of the most humble. He gave them hope even when they felt life seemed hopeless.

Two people felt that all was lost. They could have plummeted into debt with frightening consequences, but Elisha showed them just how much God cared for them. For God, minor things can have major implications. God is never too busy to care about His people, and He never overlooks how important little things can be.

HE WILL TAKE MY SONS AS SLAVES!

How could this happen to her? Her husband had been a good man who revered the Lord (2 Kings 4:1). He had been in the company of the prophets. Now after his death, his widow faced a creditor who threatened to take her two sons as slaves to pay an outstanding debt. The creditor had a legal right because slavery was a valid provision in the Law of Moses for repaying debt. Those in debt would remain as slaves until the family could pay the debt or they were eventually freed in the year of Jubilee or seventh sabbath year (Deuteronomy 15:12-18). Any of these possibilities might take many years, perhaps until the children were grown.

As a widow, she faced immense obstacles. She did not have today's options of bankruptcy, life insurance, or her husband's Social

49

Security benefits. Since her husband could not serve as her male protector, she was economically dependent on society. She had no social or political status and was considered like the homeless in our culture today.

Even with all these obstacles, the Law of Moses made provisions for a widow in her situation. She was supposed to wear special widow's clothes so that others would know she was a widow and treat her accordingly (Genesis 38:14). Her cloak could not be confiscated as a pledge for a loan because she might need it as a blanket in the night (Deuteronomy 24:17). She had the right to glean any remaining harvest in fields and orchards to stretch her supply of food (Deuteronomy 24:19-22).

She was also entitled to a portion of the tithe of the "third year," which was shared with the Levite, alien, and fatherless, so that all these people would be treated equally with landowners blessed by the harvest (Deuteronomy 14:28-29). She was considered to be under God's special care, with God as her special defender (Psalm 146:9). In fact, a curse was placed on anyone who withheld justice from the alien, fatherless, or widow (Deuteronomy 27:19).

But the widow needed help now. She could not wait to take advantage of these blessings and provisions. If her sons were taken from her for any length of time, she would indeed be in perilous straits. She cried to Elisha for help.

JUST A LITTLE OIL

As a true servant of the Lord, Elisha answered her request with a question directed at her specific need: "What shall I do for you?" (2 Kings 4:2). It was like he was asking, "What do you need God to do through me?" Then he targeted it even more with, "Tell me, what do you have in your house?" Someone overhearing the conversation might have wondered why he suddenly wanted an inventory of what was in her house. Imagine being asked to give an inventory of your house, even if it was just the kitchen pantry!

But the widow knew Elisha had a plan to help. In essence, he was asking her about the resources with which she had to work. Sadly, she didn't have much to report. She replied that she had nothing except a jar of oil.

A jar of oil might seem like a small thing to us, but at that time, few products would be more indispensable than the oil she had in her home. No doubt this was olive oil, the multi-use oil of that time that took the place of butter, vegetable fat, and salad oil that we use in cooking today. In Bible times it was mixed with grain before it was baked or sometimes spread over dough. Olive oil was also burned as fuel for torches and lamps, and it was used in rituals for the priesthood, kingship, and sacrifices.[1]

This "do-it-all" oil was used as food, fuel, medicine, and ointment, and just about everyone needed it. It was considered a valuable commodity. Because it was time-consuming to produce, it was expensive. In fact, it was like gold or money. She just had a jar of oil, but that was all God needed. Elisha knew how important just a little could be in His hands.

Elisha asked the widow to go and ask all her neighbors for empty jars (2 Kings 4:3). Then he added that she should get as many as she could. As she scurried from neighbor to neighbor, can't you see them wondering, *Just how many jars do three people need anyway?*

Elisha's request allowed her to do something to help herself and her children in their predicament. She and her sons had to work to obtain all the jars they could find. She obeyed Elisha's directions, taking a leap of faith and trusting without knowing exactly what would happen. She just knew God was leading the prophet, and that was enough.

Then she followed Elisha's next request: to close the door behind her and her sons and then pour her oil into all the jars that had been collected. When the last jar was full, the oil stopped flowing. She reported this to Elisha, and he told her to sell the oil, pay her debts from the earnings, and live on what was left. Not only were her sons active participants in this miracle, but her neighbors no doubt also witnessed God's power to turn a little oil into many jars of oil for her to live on. We can only imagine her amazement at what God could do with such a little thing and her joy at knowing how much He cared for her and her sons.

WORKDAY AT THE RIVER

In 2 Kings 6:1, Elisha helped a man who had a similar problem as the widow—debt with its possible disastrous implications. He too, like the widow's husband, was a son of the prophets. This meant he had been training to be a prophet in the guild called the sons or company of the prophets.

The prophet Samuel first started a school for prophets at Ramah (1 Samuel 19:19-20). Centuries later these schools flourished at Bethel, Jericho, Gilgal, and elsewhere (2 Kings 2:3,5; 4:38, 6:1). It is possible that the 100 prophets whom Obadiah hid in two caves from Jezebel's threats of death were a part of this group (1 Kings 18:3-4). At least 50 were near Bethel and Jericho when Elijah was transported to heaven (2 Kings 2:7). Though not all prophets attended schools like these, many formed colonies in religious training centers where a leader taught them the law and its interpretation. They then taught the people, denounced their sins, and served as spiritual leaders in a hostile, ungodly culture (1 Kings 20:35-42; 2 Kings 17:13).[2]

More prophets seemed to be joining their ranks because one of these groups was growing out of the building where Elisha was visiting. They suggested to the prophet that they move near the Jordan River. There each man could cut down a pole, and together, they could build a bigger place. Elisha approved the plan.

Then one of them asked Elisha to join them at the worksite. Perhaps they wanted him there for his approval, moral support, and blessing from God. This showed their love and appreciation for him, their mentor. It also gave him the opportunity to see how these men worked together in a different setting.

Soon the religious scholars were demonstrating their brawn as they chopped away at the trees to construct their meeting place. They probably built the building of poles from trees in the Jordan Valley, most likely with the acacia, willow, and tamarisk wood found there. Their hard work and creative solution to their problem also demonstrated their humility in seeking a simple, rustic place to gather.

LOSING THE AXE HEAD

Many people might think what happened next was trivial. They may even question why it is in the Bible. They reason that everyone loses something every day and wonder, *Why did Elisha perform a miracle to retrieve it?*

As one of the sons of the prophets was slinging his axe, the axe head came off and fell in the water. With the insecure fastening plus the bluntness of primitive axes, this was no doubt, a common occurrence. Most axe heads at this time were lashed to the shaft by leather cords. Although iron was becoming more available by this time, the iron axe head was still expensive and valuable. If it was lost, the replacement cost could have been staggering.

The man immediately cried out to Elisha that it was borrowed. The man took his responsibility seriously. He knew that if he didn't find the axe head, he could end up a slave if he didn't have the money to replace it. His future looked grim.

As with the poor widow, Elisha asked a question: "Where did it fall?" After the prophet threw a stick at the place where the man indicated, the heavy iron head floated on the water. Can you imagine the sight this must have been to any workers nearby who saw it? Then Elisha simply told the man to lift it out, and the man complied. What a story about the power of God to tell at their next meal together! He does care for His people, even in the little things.

GOD IS IN THE DETAILS

Elisha vividly demonstrated that God was in the details when he helped the alarmed widow and fearful prophet-in-training. It was more than just increasing a little oil in a jar or finding a lost axe head. Each calamity meant possible slavery to pay back a debt. God cared for these people, and He wanted them to know it through Elisha.

We have heard that "God is in the details," but we often don't live like we believe it. We wonder if *He* really cares about *our* details. We think, *That isn't important enough to pray about or God is too busy to hear about my insignificant problems. Does He really care about my committee presentation, my pounding headache, or my lost keys?*

Sometimes the details that seem trivial to us turn out not to be as insignificant as we thought. When we see God helping us in minor difficulties, it reminds us that He cares for us even in the everyday circumstances and seemingly small things of life. If we learn to trust God in the small things, we can trust Him when times get tough and our problems seem greater than we can handle. They might be big, but He is bigger.

SMALL THINGS WITH AMAZING RESULTS

Some people in the Old Testament had some pretty big problems. God took the small things they had, along with their faith, and did some awesome things. God can use the little things we have and do some extraordinary things, too.

- Jochebed saved her son, Moses, by putting him in a papyrus *basket* in the Nile where Pharaoh's daughter found and adopted him (Exodus 2:3).

- Moses parted the Red Sea with his *staff* so that the Israelites could walk through on dry land, and the Egyptians were later drowned (Exodus 14:27-31).

- Rahab, the prostitute, tied a scarlet *cord* in the window over the wall to later save herself and her family as she helped the Israelite spies to escape from Jericho (Joshua 2:15-21; Hebrews 11:31: James 2:25).

- The judge, Shamgar, saved Israel by striking down 600 Philistines with an *oxgoad,* a wooden pole with a spade at one end and a sharp point for prodding oxen at the other (Judges 3:31).

- When Gideon and his army broke their *jars* over *torches* and blew their *trumpets,* their enemy, the Midianites, started fighting with each other. The Israelites pursued them and were victorious (Judges 7:15-22).

- Samson killed 1,000 Philistines with a donkey's *jawbone* (Judges 15:15).

- David slew Goliath, a giant over nine feet tall with a *sling* and a *stone* (1 Samuel 17:50).

The Apostle Paul clearly saw that God used the weak and small things that people had to demonstrate His mighty power, for God's "power is made perfect in weakness" (2 Corinthians 12:9, ESV). Nowhere is this seen more clearly than in the ministry of Jesus.

JESUS AND THE LITTLE THINGS
God's miraculous power was seen most evidently in His Son, Jesus. Whether it was the fishes and loaves of a little boy feeding thousands, the water in jars turning into wine, or the two mites serving as an example of generous giving to generations, Jesus took little things and multiplied the results.

When His people trust and obey His Word, the Lord will bless the small things they do, so He can do great things through them. In fact, it is in doing little things that we become more like Christ. Jesus specialized in doing "small jobs," the tasks that nobody wanted to do like washing dirty feet, touching "unclean" lepers, and getting up early to fix a breakfast for His friends. He took on these jobs, not in spite of, but *because* He was God's Son (John 13:3-5). He calls us to follow His example (John 13:15). As author Rick Warren writes,

No task is beneath you when you have a servant's heart. Great opportunities often disguise themselves in small tasks. The little things in life determine the big things. Don't look for great tasks to do for God. Just do the not-so-great stuff, and God will assign you whatever he wants you to do. There will always be more people willing to do 'great' things for God than there are people willing to do the little things. The race to be a leader is crowded, but the field is wide open for those willing to be servants. Sometimes you serve upward to those in authority, and sometimes you serve downward to those in need. Either way, you develop a servant's heart when you're willing to do anything needed.[2]

Sounds a lot like Elisha, doesn't it?

GOING FURTHER

1. What were the economic implications if the widow lost her sons to slavery for several years?
2. What were the benefits for the widow and her neighbors in asking for jars? How could the miracle have impacted her sons?
3. How do you think the widow and her sons could live on what was left? What could they have learned in the process of the miracle to help them do this?
4. Why do you think God used what the woman already had to multiply and bless her? What can we learn from her for our own lives?
5. How did God defend the cause of the widow in this miracle (Deuteronomy 10:18)? On what other occasions in the Bible did God act to defend widows?
6. What qualities do you see in the sons of the prophets during their workday?

7. Why would some people consider the miracle of the axe head trivial? How is it important?
8. What are some ways that "God is in the details" of our lives? How does God's attention to the little things show us He cares?
9. How did some people in the Bible demonstrate that God's "power is made perfect in weakness" (2 Corinthians 12:9)?
10. What are ways Jesus specialized in "small jobs"? How does His example translate to our lives today?

WHO ELSE?

Who else miraculously produced more liquid than was needed in a crisis (John 2:1-11)?

A LEAP OF FAITH: BEING A BIBLE SCHOOL BUDDY

For years, Natalie Reed had felt that God was calling her for a special ministry in her congregation. She took a leap of faith and decided to be a "buddy" for two children of families who worship with her. One of these children is a five-year-old named Taft, who lives with autism spectrum disorder.

Taft enjoyed Bible class, but sometimes he became overstimulated by all the sights and sounds. He would feel anxious and overwhelmed and need to leave his class. Since he was too old for the nursery, there would be no place for him to go, except home or an empty classroom. Though there were once few alternatives, now he is more likely to stay in his class with his buddy, Natalie.

Natalie's congregation doesn't want these special needs children to be forgotten or ignored. The church assigns a buddy to stay with special needs children during Bible class. This serves the entire family by giving the parents an opportunity to attend their own Bible class, a rare treat since their children require full-time attention and supervision. Natalie encourages others to consider such a ministry: "You don't have to have a degree in special education...You just have to have the heart to serve and the willingness to sit with and help the children in Bible class." [3]

The consistency and routine of having an understanding buddy alongside to help and encourage have been a blessing to Taft and Natalie. She explains, "The families I have met through this ministry have meant more to me and touched my heart more than words can express...I may have signed up to help them, but God has used them to bless and help me more than they know." [4]

CHERISHING FRIENDSHIPS

2 Kings 4:8-37

Can you think of someone you would like to have as a houseguest on a regular, rotating basis? You are fortunate if you do. Many people cringe when they hear that company is coming. They grin and bear their "intruders," especially when their guests stay too long, talk too much, and eat them out of house and home. No wonder some hostesses agree with Benjamin Franklin: "Fish and visitors smell after three days." [1]

However, can you imagine people who would *build on a room* so someone could stay with them whenever he passed through town? Not only that, but they provided the amenities to make it comfortable and welcoming so he would want to come back. Even more amazing, after their visitor came and went regularly, they still remained good friends. What a hospitable host and hostess!

REST FOR A TRAVELING MAN

Elisha was a man on the go. In fact, he spent most of his time prophesying, teaching, and counseling, while traveling a circuit in Israel. As he passed through Shunem, a town north of Jezreel in Israel, a wealthy woman invited him to stay for a meal (2 Kings 4:8). It was a tradition at that time when people ate together, they were no longer strangers but formed a bond of friendship that should not be broken. There was "bread and salt between them." [2] So whenever Elisha came through Shunem, he was a welcome guest in her home.

The Shunammite woman recognized Elisha as a holy "man of God" (2 Kings 4:9). This title of honor signified a few of God's prophets who were extraordinarily close to God and had a powerful spiritual prophetic gift. (Elisha was called a "man of God" more than 25 times in the Bible.) The woman wanted to provide a private place for Elisha to pray and rest whenever he visited.

She asked her husband if they could extend their hospitality further by providing a small room on their roof, including a bed, table, chair and lamp. Such furnishings were better than poorer homes where people slept on mats on the floor or sat cross-legged on the floor to eat. Most beds at that time were not like our plush mattresses today. They consisted of heavy mats over cords stretched across wooden frames, but they were better than sleeping on the floor!

A GIFT IN RETURN

Elisha appreciated the woman's hospitality so much that he told his servant, Gehazi, to ask her what he could do for her. Elisha had enough influence in Israel that he offered to put in a good word for her with the king or commander of the army. Elisha knew these two most powerful people in the land well enough for them to fulfill his request if he asked them. The Shunammite woman answered that she had a home among her own people. She was content.

Gehazi observed what the prophet had missed: The woman had no children, and her husband was old, probably beyond childbearing age. In those days, if a husband died and the wife had no children, she would have no protector or provider to care for her in old age. No one would be there to carry on the family name. Others would inherit her family possessions and land.

Elisha told her that about the same time next year, she would hold a son in her arms. She asked Elisha not to mislead her. She didn't want to put her hopes in something that seemed impossible. Her reaction was understandable in a Jewish culture that felt childlessness was a curse from God. The Jews believed parents lived on in their offspring and the more children the better (Psalm 127:3-5).

Although all babies were a cause for joy, boys were considered a special blessing. In that culture, when they grew up, they stayed at home, supporting the family and increasing its size with wives and children, while girls grew up to leave home when they married. No wonder the Shunammite woman thought Elisha's prophecy was too good to be true. But through the power of God, she bore a son at the time Elisha had predicted.

"MY HEAD. MY HEAD"
Several years passed, and one day the son went out to his father in the fields with the reapers. The boy complained of a headache, saying "My head, my head," and the father asked a servant to take his son to his mother (2 Kings 4:19). Many scholars think that perhaps the boy had been too long in the sun and suffered from sunstroke. Others think that he could have had meningitis, cerebral malaria, or a cerebral hemorrhage.[3] For whatever reason, the child died later at noon on his mother's lap.

Instead of plummeting into grief and initiating preparations for his burial, she did what might seem a curious thing. She purposely placed the child on Elisha's bed in his upstairs room and then shut the door. By doing this, she could conceal the child's death from others while she hurried in her preparations to leave. Calling to her husband, she asked for a donkey and servant to accompany her to go see Elisha quickly and return. She didn't mention their son was dead.

Her husband was perplexed because she intended to visit Elisha when it was not the New Moon or the Sabbath. This implies that previously she may have worshipped where Elisha had ministered or spoken on those days. Perhaps to lessen her husband's concern, she told him, "It will be well" (2 Kings 4:23).

She felt the need to share her news only with Elisha. After cherishing her son whose birth Elisha had foretold, she must have struggled with his sudden death. She sought help from the only man she felt could do anything about it. She saddled a donkey and told her servant to quickly lead the animal to Mount Carmel where Elisha was. She was determined to reach Elisha as quickly as possible.

Now Elisha was perplexed. From his vantage point at Mount Carmel, he could see the woman approaching in the distance, and he wondered what could have prompted her 20-mile journey from Shunem. Elisha asked Gehazi to run and meet her to ask if she and her family were all right. When Gehazi reached her and asked, she answered him, "It is well" (2 Kings 4:26).

When she finally arrived where Elisha was, she cast her dignity aside and grasped his feet as a gesture of entreaty and humility. Gehazi was ready to push her away when Elisha told him that God had not revealed her distress to him. The woman entreated Elisha, "Did I ask for a son from my lord? Did I not say, 'Do not deceive me?'" (2 Kings 4:28).

Immediately, Elisha perceived her anguish and told Gehazi to run, tucking his cloak in his belt and refusing to greet anyone on the way. These practical steps would prevent anything from slowing him down. Elisha directed Gehazi to take the prophet's staff and put it on the boy's face, probably since it was the boy's head that hurt. Elisha saw his staff as his own presence, serving as a symbol of God's divine power, rather than a magical charm.

The woman was not willing to leave Elisha or wait for the child to respond via long distance. So Elisha followed her back to her home, as Gehazi ran on ahead. Gehazi must have been tired of running! He followed Elisha's instructions, but there was no sound or response. Gehazi went back and told Elisha of his failed attempt to rouse the cold corpse.

Elisha and the woman eventually reached her home, and Elisha went in alone with the boy. The prophet prayed and then stretched his body across the lifeless boy with their eyes, mouth, and hands touching. The boy's body began to grow warm. Elisha paced some more and then stretched himself on the boy again. Then the boy began to sneeze... and sneeze... and sneeze. This proved that his breath was returning. Elisha was not using resuscitation via artificial respiration, but prayerfully asking God to raise the boy from death to life.

After sneezing seven times, the boy came to life and opened his eyes. Elisha called Gehazi to summon the woman and Elisha told her, "Take up your son" (2 Kings 4:36). In grateful praise, she fell at his feet and bowed to the ground. Elisha represented God to her. It was God who had given her a son in such a special way, and He had the power to also bring her son back from the dead. She took a leap of faith in believing that God could do the impossible. And He did!

SAVING THE FAMILY FARM AFTER FAMINE

The raising of her son was not the only thing for which the Shunammite woman could praise God. God also worked through Elisha to save her family farm. Because of Israel's disobedience, God sent a seven-year famine, twice as long as the previous one (2 Kings 8:1: Luke 4:25). Elisha warned the women to leave Israel during this period. She believed Elisha and decided to take her son and household to the land of the Philistines. Philistia on the flood plain of the Mediterranean Coast would be a better place to weather out the famine.

At the end of the famine, the woman returned to find her land confiscated. Because the land had been deserted, ownership would have reverted to the king. Or was this king possibly like the earlier king Ahab, who grabbed up land to his advantage (1 Kings 21)? Since she had to reclaim the land on behalf of her son, who would be the rightful heir, her husband had probably died. At the very time she was to make her appeal to the king, Elisha's servant, Gehazi, was telling the king about this woman and the raising of her son. It was no accident that she appeared at the same moment. The king not only returned the land, but also commanded that she be reimbursed for the back income. God accomplished His purpose even in her circumstances.

NURTURING "GO TO" FRIENDS

The Shunammite woman probably didn't realize it when she first invited Elisha to share a meal with her and her husband that they had found a "go to" friend. Such a friend is one of the first people you think of when you experience joy, sorrow, or trouble. You call on them because you have to let them know. You know they will care. They are the first ones you "go to."

This threesome was richly blessed to enjoy one another's company. What a comfort for Elisha to kick off his dusty sandals and relax with close friends at the end of a weary day of traveling. They, in turn, were blessed by his words from God and the stories of God's mighty works. These friends shared some mutual traits that made their devotion to one another extraordinary.

Thoughtfulness — After several occasions of Elisha's stopping by to eat with them, the woman thought ahead, suggesting to her husband how a furnished room would serve the prophet well in his role. Elisha thought ahead as well and asked if he could speak on her behalf to the king or commander.

Do we think ahead about how we can serve our friends in their daily lives? How can we surprise them by making their days easier or happier?

Gratitude — The woman and her husband appreciated the good work that Elisha was doing so, they invested in that work by providing hospitality whenever he was in town. Elisha, in turn, so appreciated their gift of hospitality that he promised them a son through the Lord's grace.

How do we show appreciation to our friends just for being there for us? Do we often let them know how much we care about them?

Loyalty — Even though the woman was heartbroken and frustrated, she was loyal to Elisha by not denouncing him to others when her child died. Instead she hurried to find the prophet at Mount Carmel so that he could do something about the situation. Likewise, Elisha was loyal to her when he warned her to leave the country to avoid the impending seven-year famine.

Are we loyal to our friends? Do we defend them when they are unjustly criticized or mistreated? Do we protect their privacy when others pry?

Respect — The woman honored Elisha by calling him a "holy man of God" and bowing before him. In respect for her, Elisha quickly acted on her request for help when he learned that her child had died.

Do we respect our friend's time and energy when we ask for favors? Do we show them respect by listening to what they have to say before we speak?

Persistence — The woman didn't give up in seeking Elisha's help when her son died. After she found him, she would not leave him until he personally went to raise her son. When Gehazi was unsuccessful at raising the boy, Elisha prayed and tried several times until the child sneezed, coming to life.

Do we keep trying to cheer and support our friends when they become discouraged or seriously ill? Do we show them we won't give up on them?

Solomon wrote about a godly bond of friendship like Elisha and the Shunammite couple when he observed, "Two are better than one because they have a good return for their labor. For if either of them falls, the one will lift up his companion. But woe to the one who falls when there is not another to lift him up... A cord of three strands is not quickly torn apart" (Ecclesiastes 4:9-10, 12).

FINDING AND KEEPING "GO TO" FRIENDS

Finding "go to" friends is a challenge in our hectic lives. But friendships should be a priority because they don't thrive on autopilot. Make yourself accessible. Get out and "go to" where people are. Be open to opportunities.

Recharge your spiritual battery with someone in a Bible study, prayer group, or other ministry group in your congregation. Get to know another parent by getting involved with your children's class and activities at school. Ask someone to join you walking, running, or taking an exercise/martial arts class. Reconnect with a former classmate, co-worker, or club member and make some new memories.

Reach out to someone you would like to know better. Get her phone number or email address. Invite her to join you to do something fun. Share an adventure together — a new play, an art lesson, a kayak trip. Getting together doesn't have to involve a lot of money or planning. Meet up for a bagel, latte, or ice cream cone. Take dinner to her house and eat it together.

Most women will be flattered to be asked to join you. It might take several invitations to be able to get together, but keep asking. (Just don't stalk her.) However, if someone is not interested, you can find someone else who is. Perhaps that woman was not the right fit for you. Don't give up.

Focus on finding a few good friends. We all have limitations of time and energy. The reality is that we can't be best friends with everyone. Remember, Jesus had friends and knew many people. However, He chose to focus on 12 men. Within that group, He had three close friends: Peter, James, and John. They were His "go to" friends (Proverbs 18:24).

GOING FURTHER

1. What about the Shunammite woman would make you want to be her friend? What qualities did Elisha possess that could have made him a welcome guest?
2. Why do you think the woman chose to include the furniture she put in her guest room for Elisha? How did her gift of hospitality to Elisha bring rich rewards?
3. What do you observe about the husband's faith and attitudes? Why do you think he sent the sick child to be with his mother?
4. How do you think the woman could tell her husband and Gehazi, "It will be well," in the most heartbreaking of circumstances?
5. How did the woman show her determination and persistence to go to Elisha after her son was dead?

6. Why do you think Elisha initially sent his staff instead of going himself? Why do you think Gehazi's attempt to raise the son didn't work?

7. What are some of the qualities you see in your friends that make them special? What are some ways they demonstrate these qualities?

8. Have you ever had a friendship that began with sharing a meal together? How does eating together foster relationships?

9. What are some ways that you can make new friends where you live? How can you help others to make new friends?

10. What can we learn from Jesus' example about having friends? Who were some other good friends of Jesus?

WHO ELSE?

Who else raised a dead child after a parent requested help (Mark 5:35-43)?

A LEAP IN FAITH: MENTORING WITH THE CONNECTION PROJECT

Women often want to develop meaningful relationships with other women in the church, but they don't know where to start. Some 20-somethings took the initiative to simplify the process of mentoring to connect younger and older women.

Twenty-two-year-old Kayla Barker Martinez saw a need to encourage younger women in their upper teens, 20s, and 30s. With the help of other women, Kayla and her friend, Alison James, took a leap of faith and co-coordinated a Young Women's Seminar in their congregation. The theme for the event was "Answering the Call of Titus 2." The seminar stressed that younger women as well as older ones have a responsibility to get to know and learn from one another.

An outgrowth of the seminar was the Connection Project, which seeks to initiate the mentoring ideas discussed in the seminar. A kickoff was held for all those interested. Everyone wrote on an index card the names of two or three who were attending (or possibly someone else interested in the congregation) with whom they would like to be paired. Kayla and Alison paired the cards, and all were given a list of suggested activities they could enjoy together. At a later meeting, they compared notes, sharing their experiences and how they had grown.

Among other activities, Kayla and her mentor went out to lunch, went to the mall, and took lunch to an elderly couple. They also learned from another older lady in the church's Dorcas group how to sew a simple skirt to send to little girls in Haiti. Commenting on their activities, Kayla observed, "It's been such fun! The age gap isn't what matters. It's the connection made." [4]

FEASTING IN A FAMILY

2 Kings 4:38-44

Whether you are an introvert or extrovert, solitude can be beneficial. Spending time alone can be restorative and bolster your creativity. It isn't healthy, however, to be isolated from others for too long. In fact, it can be scary!

Remember Elisha's mentor, Elijah, felt so alone and discouraged that he asked God to let him die. Elijah's feeling of isolation from other followers of God made him feel like he was the only one serving the Almighty. The Lord's reminder that 7,000 others were faithful was comforting to Elijah. It was good to know he wasn't serving God solo. What truly must have given his faith a jumpstart was sharing fellowship with a godly friend like Elisha and other "prophets-in-training."

Elisha seemed to take the same comfort in community. His work with the sons of the prophets not only encouraged them but also bolstered his own faith. These prophets must have also enjoyed close fellowship with each other. After all, they learned together, ate together, and worked together for common goals just like a family. In times of famine, they found it necessary to stretch their resources together. But on two occasions, it was only the Lord's providence that turned what could have become a family fiasco at mealtime into a family feast.

BEING FED IN FAMINE

You know a famine was bad when King Ahab and his servant, Obadiah, were out combing the countryside for grass! Before the Mount Carmel contest, they were forced to go look for grass for the royal horses and mules, so they wouldn't have to slaughter them (1 Kings 18:5). Israel's economy depended on agriculture. Their necessities of life, like food, clothing, and shelter, were derived from the land. With their daily needs in short supply, Israel should have looked to God to provide, but instead they relied on Baal.

Perhaps in a desperate attempt to appease Baal so that he would send rain and end the famine, Queen Jezebel was killing the prophets of God. To rescue them, Obadiah was secretly hiding 100 prophets in two caves and providing them food and water (1 Kings 18:13-14). That had to be quite an operation, especially since Obadiah was accomplishing it right under Ahab's nose!

As time went on, a more frightening famine threatened Israel—a spiritual dearth of godliness as Israel starved for God and His Word. Fortunately, there were young men eagerly hungering and thirsting after righteousness, and they craved teaching and counsel. Communities of prophets sprang up in opposition to the apostasy and indifference in the people around them. These sons of the prophets were attracted by the dynamic ministries of Elijah and Elisha. From their mentors, they were challenged to learn more of the Word of God. No doubt manifestations of God's power through the prophets were retold and preserved by these younger prophets to share with others.

Elisha could have stayed in the comfort of his home, especially at this time of a later famine, possibly the same seven-year famine that prompted the Shunammite women to leave her home (2 Kings 4:38; 8:1).[1] Instead he chose to travel, visiting certain towns in Israel where the schools of the prophets were thriving. One such company of these prophets was at Gilgal. At this time, the prophets were meeting with Elisha, most likely to listen to him teach.

Elisha knew how the famine affected his students and that they would need a warm, hearty meal. So he told his servant to put a large pot on the fire and make some stew for them. Into such a stew went all kinds of ingredients to stretch what was available. So "Mulligan Stew" was on the menu, and Elisha's servant was to be the chef.

"MULLIGAN STEW" ON THE MENU

One of the prophets gathered herbs to season the stew and make it go further in such hard times. He found a wild vine he couldn't identify and gathered some of its gourds in the fold of his cloak. When he returned, no one else knew what the gourds were either. He cut them up and put them in the stew. Maybe he figured what they didn't know wouldn't hurt them!

When it was time to eat, the stew was served. Whether it was the taste, texture, or look of the gourd pieces, the prophets cried out, "O man of God, there is death in the pot!" (2 Kings 4:40). They couldn't eat the rest of it. This was especially bad news in a famine when the whole pot was ruined because of some poisonous gourds.

The gourds are thought to have been a yellow fruit known as wild cucumber, which must have looked edible. Its vines still grow in the region of the Dead Sea today and are known as the apples of Sodom.[2] When the fruit is dried to a powder, it can induce vomiting and is fatal in large doses.[3] No wonder the prophets didn't want to finish it.

Elisha wanted to save the stew from being thrown out and wasted, so he added flour to the pot. Miraculously, it was then safe to eat. Since flour was considered a symbol of daily provision and healing, it was an appropriate ingredient to add to the stew. But it wasn't the flour or Elisha but God who made it edible. It took a leap of faith for the prophets to eat what just a few minutes before had been sickening. They had to trust the word of the prophet from God. That miracle of the poisoned stew spoke more of God's provision for His people than any words Elisha spoke that day.

THE BLESSING OF FIRSTFRUITS

On another occasion, a man presented Elisha with an ordinary gift:20 loaves of barley bread baked from the first ripe grain, along with some heads of new grain (2 Kings 4:42). The bread was probably baked in flat, round loaves. This donation was from the firstfruits of his barley harvest, which usually came in March or April in Israel. With such a sampling of the harvest, perhaps the famine in Israel was over by this time.

This faithful follower of God traveled from a city named Baal Shalishah, which was a place located in the central hill country of Israel, where years before, Saul and his servant had looked for lost donkeys (1 Samuel 9:4). The name itself was compounded with the name Baal to form Baal Shalishah. A shrine to Baal had likely since been erected there, honoring Baal for the harvest. But this farmer knew better. He knew that the true God was Yahweh, and He had provided the harvest, as well as the seed, the soil, and the rain that brought it.

The man's gift tells us something about the giver. Barley cost half as much as wheat (2 Kings 7:1). Barley was the "poor man's bread," the bread of the poor in the villages. City dwellers preferred wheat bread. They considered barley as forage for horses, donkeys, and cattle. The gift implies that the giver might not have been wealthy. He brought what he had, and God could multiply it. He had a generous heart, and his gift filled an immediate need.

This gift of the firstfruits, the first and best of the harvest, was considered sacred. It was usually reserved for God and the Levitical priests for their support (Deuteronomy 18:4-5). The priests and Levites had no land inheritance because God had chosen them to minister to the people. They would have no extra time to work the land, so the people supported them through their offerings.

Perhaps the donor took his firstfruits to Elisha instead because at that time, he considered Elisha as God's true representative. He might have refused to offer his gifts to the priests at Dan and Bethel (1 Kings 12:28-31). This could have been his way of protesting against the apostate religion and Baal worship in the Northern Kingdom. The giver was faithful to God and the Law of Moses. In a spiritually starving nation, this farmer, in his own way, was opposing Baal and doing his part to provide a feast for God's family.

This seemingly ordinary gift was truly significant because firstfruits were given to thank God for His goodness and to acknowledge that all crops come from Him. Whether they were offered from individuals or the nation as a whole, they served as a sign of faith (Deuteronomy 26:1-11). They were considered a pledge of the harvest to come. Through the firstfruits, the giver demonstrated that he believed in God's covenant and that more blessings would follow because God was faithful in keeping His promises.

MORE THAN ENOUGH

What an opportunity this gift gave Elisha! He could use this generous gesture as a chance to encourage and strengthen the sons of the prophets not only physically, but also spiritually. The gift might have been intended for Elisha, but instead he offered it to share with them. He commanded his servant to give the grain and loaves to the crowd.

His servant objected, asking, "What, will I set this before a hundred men?" referring to the crowd of the prophets gathered there (1 Kings 4:43). Scripture does not indicate whether Gehazi was Elisha's servant at this time. We wonder how long this servant had been with Elisha and how many of the mighty works of God had he seen the prophet perform.

Elisha repeated his instruction to distribute the food, confirming that they would eat and have some left over. The servant gave out the food and just as the Lord had told Elisha, some was left over. It was important for the sons of the prophets to know that Elisha was their leader and what God could do through him. Those who enjoyed this feast saw dramatically how God not only supplied their needs, but He also gave them even more than they needed. They experienced firsthand that when God gives, He gives more than enough.

NEEDING EACH OTHER

What would it have been to shadow Elisha as he traveled to visit the sons of the prophets? With Elisha serving as their spiritual mentor, they, in turn, strengthened him and one another. They all needed one another.

Just like Elisha did then, we all need one another today. Years ago, our society was anchored in the family. Women of multiple generations lived in close proximity and shared life together. Now, our society is individualistic. We are more independent. People move several times in a lifetime, and family members live far away. We make friends, but in our mobile society, those connections are often short-lived and shallow.

In the church, this disconnection and individualism rears its ugly head in our relationships with others. When someone asks us how we are, we answer, "Fine," but know we really aren't. Someone has defined that answer of "fine" as "feelings inside never expressed." We would like to be honest with people who really care about and love us. But we also feel embarrassed to share our personal lives, and we don't want to dump our emotional baggage on casual acquaintances.

But aren't we as Christians called to share one another's burdens? Isn't that how we fulfill the law of Christ (Galatians 6:2)? God didn't create us to go through life alone, but also to have fellowship with Him and with others in His family. We were designed as community projects. Yet we struggle, trying to get along on our own, and settling for on-the-surface relationships that don't have any depth.

We are not alone in our struggle. Social scientists have found in large-scale research studies that the greatest social epidemic in American life is loneliness. According to research presented before the 2017 American Psychological Association, in the United States approximately 42.6 million adults over the age of 45 suffer from chronic loneliness, while more than a quarter of the entire American population lives alone. Trends like these suggest we are becoming less socially connected, which can have a significant risk of premature death.[4] We can see how crucial it is for us to connect with others.

BEING A PART OF A GROUP

Connecting in a one-to-one friendship is essential, but so is finding a group of friends you can call your own. Belonging to a group can make you feel a part of something bigger than yourself, especially if you are working toward a common goal. Groups can anchor you and make you feel liked and accepted. The group doesn't dissolve like a one-friend relationship would if one moves away. So how do you find a group that "fits"?

Start in your congregation. What better way to get to know others than by visiting over dinner with a bunch of women in a restaurant in a Mix and Mingle Dinner or Ladies' Night Out? Discover what common talents and interests you all have. Some churches have organized mentoring groups of younger and older ladies meeting together in homes and sharing marriage, homemaking, and parenting principles based on Titus 2. Other women share fellowship over a meal in groups and then study the Bible. Such groups like these can be engaging ways to share wisdom and biblical truths. British author C. S. Lewis, who was a member of a writer's group himself, wrote, "The next best thing to being wise oneself is to live in a circle of those who are." [5]

Some women's groups sew lap quilts for the elderly, knit scarves for soldiers, and send stamped handmade cards to the sick. When they meet, they also share prayer requests as they work on their crafts. Women find that as they talk about all kinds of things, they relax and begin to trust others with what is in their hearts.

You don't have to limit yourself to friends in the church. There might be a group in your own neighborhood. It is worth the effort to build solid relationships with those who live near you. You might be surprised at how many people might be interested in a Fourth of July block party, "Brisket Brunch," or "Burgers and Board Games." Instead of worrying about picture-perfect homes, it's a time to enjoy our friends and families, put away our phones, and talk face-to-face. You never know whom you might reach for Christ by getting to know her better.

Don't forget the groups in your community. An initial Google search will help you find almost any type of group. Some groups are just for fun, others take on projects for good causes, and some combine both. If a group doesn't interest you, consider starting your own group. You can tweak an idea that might work better for you. Some women, for example, never seemed to be able to read the book for their book club, so they opted for reading interesting longer articles. Another group loved to eat, but dreaded cleaning the house and preparing dinner for a supper club, so they chose to check out new restaurants. These friendships work both ways. You need the members of your group, but they need you, too!

GOING FURTHER

1. What are some advantages of solitude? How can it be physically and spiritually detrimental if someone remains isolated for too long?

2. How did the spiritual fellowship go both ways with Elisha and sons of the prophets? What can we learn from them about growing spiritually?

3. How did Ahab and Obadiah deal with the crisis of an earlier famine? What did Jezebel do to God's prophets during this time? How did Obadiah rescue 100 of them in spite of the famine?

4. Why was it important for the sons of the prophets to see how God was working through Elisha?

5. How did God's people provide for one another?

6. How did the man from Baal Shalisha oppose idol worship in his own way? What was so symbolic about offering the firstfruits to God?

7. Have you ever experienced or known a family with multiple generations living close together? What advantages of family life did you see?

8. How does our individualistic, mobile society make developing close, lasting relationships difficult? What are some ways we can make enduring friendships in a society like ours?

9. Why is it hard at times to share our feelings with others? What can we do to make this sharing easier when it is appropriate?

10. Why is it vital to have group friendships as well as one-to-one friendships? What are the advantages of each?

WHO ELSE?

Who else doubted that so many people could be fed from so little (John 6:7)?

A LEAP IN FAITH: HANDCRAFTING TO MAKE IT SPECIAL

In these days of assembly line look-alikes, it is special to find something handcrafted, but even more remarkable to find someone who is willing to teach her craft to others. One lady has been teaching crafting to sisters in the church for almost two decades. At her congregation, they have formed "Helping Hands for Christ Ladies Outreach," touching thousands in their community and beyond.

Karen Dingley's love of crafting began when she learned to knit in junior high. Later when she had small children, she served by knitting and crocheting items for the "Warm Up America" program. She was challenged by a Bible teacher who asked the class how they could serve through their talents. He asked, "What do you like to do?" That spurred her on to take a leap of faith and share her love of crafting with other ladies. Her husband, Doug, the church minister, supported her in her efforts and began finding outlets for their creations.

The group meets once a week to craft an array of lovely items, such as hats, mittens, afghans, ponchos, quilts, sweaters, headbands, blankets, cancer caps, lap robes, and stuffed toys. These are donated in the name of Christ to schools, hospitals, shelters, children's homes, and treatment facilities.[6]

Everyone is welcome to join, where laughter, learning, and love of crafting make the hours go quickly. In time, Karen has taught her sisters everything from doing basic stitches to creating their own designs. She says, "It has gotten much bigger than I ever thought it would. Every time I teach someone to knit or crochet, I love to see the smile on her face when she completes that first project." [7] Anyone receiving one of the group's creations will be smiling, too!

EMBRACING HUMILITY

2 Kings 5

Sickness is a humbling experience. Just think of the last time you had the flu or possibly COVID-19. One look in the mirror said it all. You looked terrible. You felt even worse. You just knew you were going to die. The truth about any health ailment is that it is the great leveler. You can be a millionaire executive or the poorest beggar, but disease can lay both of you low. If you can't find a cure, you are in the same boat.

One successful, rich man was willing to pay the equivalent of millions of dollars for a cure. Instead, he found a free cure for both his body and soul. He only needed to humble himself.

THE NEEDY RICH MAN

Naaman was a soldier's soldier. This "Stormin' Naaman" was brave, honorable, and highly regarded by his master, the king of Aram. (Aram was also known as Syria.) Naaman was pivotal in God's plan to humble Israel "because by him the Lord had given victory to Aram" (2 Kings 5:1). This might have referred to Aram's victory over King Ahab at Ramoth Gilead (1 Kings 22:29-38). Rabbinic tradition holds that Naaman was the soldier who shot the random, but fatal, arrow that killed Ahab in that battle.[1]

With all his accomplishments and power, Naaman had something that made him feel powerless. He had some type of skin disease. The Hebrew word translated "leprosy" in this passage was used to describe several skin diseases. Naaman's disease might have been smelly, painful, and debilitating. It could have brought an aversion and disgust from others that made him feel like an outcast, even if he was not isolated by a medical or ritual quarantine. In pagan cultures, a disease like his was often seen as punishment from the gods.

It seems Naaman's disease had not yet totally isolated him because he led an army, lived at home, and had an audience with the king. Perhaps his was not a serious disease or if it were serious, it was in its initial stages. Whatever his malady, Naaman wanted to free himself of the social stigma and humiliation, as well as the disease itself.

What we do know is that Naaman suffered from his disease, and he was willing to pay a king's ransom to get well. He had heard through his Israelite slave girl that a prophet in Samaria could cure him. On one of Aram's raids on Israel, this young girl had been abducted, separated from her family, and given to Naaman's wife. In spite of how she had been treated, she exhibited extraordinary empathy for her master by telling Naaman's wife of a possible cure. She must have previously been taught about God and His prophet, Elisha.

It had to be somewhat humiliating for Naaman to take the advice of an ordinary slave girl from his enemy Israel, but he was desperate. He would try anything. In time, he would owe much more to this young lady than his healing.

NO RED CARPET FOR THE DIGNITARY

Naaman faced a sticky situation with protocol that complicated his mission. How does a military commander of Syria, who had formerly conducted raids on Israel, contact an Israelite prophet? At that time, a politically uneasy peace existed between Aram and Israel, and this called for diplomatic skill.

To solve his dilemma, Naaman visited the king of Aram. Aram's king wrote the king of Israel a letter of introduction, asking him to cure Naaman of his disease. When the king of Israel received his letter, he tore his royal robe in despair. Such an act was a sign of national tragedy or crisis. Was Aram's king thinking Israel's king could cure Naaman? Or was Aram's king trying to pick a quarrel to start a war with Israel again? Because the king of Israel relied on his own resources instead of God, he didn't consider asking Elisha for help.

Elisha heard about the king of Israel's reaction and requested that he send Naaman to him. Naaman arrived with his entourage of horses and chariots, expecting a dignitary's welcome. The prophet didn't roll out the red carpet for the distinguished commander. Instead he sent his servant, Gehazi, out to tell him to dip seven times in the Jordan River, and he would be healed.

Naaman was angered by Elisha's reception. The commander seemed to expect a hand-waving magician reciting incantations over him. When Elisha didn't do that, Naaman expected any body of water could cleanse him so why not the rushing, clear rivers of Damascus? Perhaps he thought the prophet only offered him a ritual cleansing in the Jordan River instead of total healing (2 Kings 5:12). To compound Naaman's frustration, the muddy, meandering Jordan River was about 40 miles away, and there was no direct, easy route from Samaria. Naaman's pride was wounded, and he left in a huff.

A HUMBLER NAAMAN

"Stormin' Naaman" would have huffed all the way to Aram if his servants had not asked him to stop and think. These messengers of reason asked him if Elisha had requested him to do something difficult to be healed, he would have done it. Surely he could try this simple task. Naaman thought again and decided to comply with Elisha's directions.

After he dipped in the Jordan seven times, his flesh was restored like a young boy's. He returned to Elisha a grateful and humbler man. This formerly proud, pagan Gentile now confessed, "I know that there is no God in all the earth, but in Israel; so please take a present from your servant now" (2 Kings 5:15). If only the thousands of idolatrous Israelites at that time had make the same confession.

When Elisha remained detached from the miracle, Naaman knew that it was only by the power of God that he was healed.

Naaman's healing was a free gift of grace from God. In a culture of wonder-workers and false prophets, Elisha refrained from giving any impression that he was a "prophet for hire." So Elisha refused Naaman's gifts. He was not a "for-profit prophet."

Then Naaman made an odd request. He wanted some Israeli soil to take back with him to make burnt offerings to the God of Israel. Naaman associated the land of Israel with its God so how could he worship Him on Aramean soil? He decided to transport dirt from Israel and worship the true God on an altar built of that dirt. Altars like this might have been made of mud bricks or stone walls with interiors filled with earth (Exodus 20:24).

Naaman even asked forgiveness when he had to escort his master to worship in the pagan temple of Rimmon, also known as Hadad, the god of storm and war. (The two names were sometimes combined as in Zechariah 12:11.) Elisha acknowledged Naaman's determination and told him, "Go in peace" (2 Kings 5:19). So Naaman left for Aram with God's healing, Elisha's blessing, and Israel's dirt and in the process lost his arrogance.

GEHAZI'S TIME FOR PAYBACK?

What a marvelous transformation had taken place in Naaman's body and soul! This had happened before Gehazi's very eyes, but it seems his thoughts were elsewhere. Maybe Elisha's servant was still reeling over the extravagant offer of Naaman's payment to Elisha that the prophet had refused. In today's buying power, it had an estimated worth of hundreds of millions! He could not let the opportunity pass to get "something" from this grateful man. Gehazi's covetousness and greed drove him to run after Naaman's chariot and catch up with him. Humbled by his miraculous healing, Naaman got down from the chariot and asked Gehazi if everything was all right.

Gehazi concocted a story, telling Naaman that Elisha had requested a talent of silver and two sets of clothing for two visiting sons of the prophets from Ephraim. When compared to Naaman's excessive offer, Gehazi's request was modest, but still sizable. Considering that in those days one talent of silver equaled about 300 years of wages, Gehazi was looking to set himself up financially and "retire" for life. [2]

Naaman doubled the silver requested along with the two sets of clothing and sent two servants with Gehazi to go back to Samaria. When Gehazi got closer to home, he dismissed the servants and then hid the contraband in the house without telling Elisha. When Elisha asked him where he had been, he answered that he hadn't gone anywhere. Elisha knew better and asked him, "Is it a time to receive money and receive clothes and olive groves and vineyards and sheep and oxen and male and female servants?" (2 Kings 5:26). Elisha's rebuke referred to the life of leisure and luxury Gehazi expected to enjoy with Naaman's generous gift.

Then Elisha dealt Gehazi a shocking blow. He and his descendants would inherit Naaman's leprosy. Gehazi left Elisha's presence as white as snow.

Why would Gehazi's greed consume him and cause him to lie and steal what did not belong to him? Gehazi, much like Judas Iscariot, had not learned much from his master. Gehazi possibly had spent 15-20 years with Elisha, seeing firsthand God's power in numerous miraculous works. Why was he so tempted by worldly blessings when he had witnessed so many eternal ones?

Did he long for some power and success himself and saw this was a way to obtain it? Or did he see an opportunity to leave the toil of service to God behind and enjoy an easy life in wealth and pleasure? Was Gehazi's vision blurred by national prejudice and pride, seeing Naaman as "the Aramean" who had looted Israelites? Did he think it was time to get some payback from a plundering enemy? Whatever the reason(s), he and his family were doomed like Naaman had been. What a price to pay for his greed!

WALKING HUMBLY WITH OUR GOD

If *Twitter* had existed in ancient Israel, it's possible that one of the popular tweets would have been "Acclaimed Syrian army hero requests dirt from Israel." The fact that a hated enemy of Israel would take its soil home with him was newsworthy. But it was also a mystery. People no doubt wondered, *Why was a powerful man like Naaman taking dirt home to Syria?*

Such news would point to how Naaman transformed from a proud commander to a humbler man who believed in God. It was all a matter of perspective for him. Naaman's heart changed when he had a better understanding of who God was and his own relationship to Him. Remember how he exclaimed to Elisha, "I know that there is no God in all the earth, but in Israel" (2 Kings 5:15). Naaman finally acknowledged that God healed him of his leprosy, He was in control, and He deserved his worship on an altar made of Israel's soil.

Naaman finally got it. So should we.

When we realize what God has done for us, it can change our perspective, too. Like Naaman, we can acknowledge that God is in control, not us. When we put God in His rightful place, we better understand where we belong. We are God's precious children who belong to Him (1 Peter 2:9). God loves us. We don't have to prove ourselves to others because God has already proven Himself in many ways. Our trust and confidence holds fast in Him.

Think about it — proud people feel they are more important than anyone else, so they trust in themselves. But the humble put their trust in God. The humble give glory to God while the proud give glory to themselves.

Humility is not feeling others are better than us; it's knowing our significance and worth are found in Christ. As evangelist Charles Spurgeon said, "Humility is to make a right estimate of one's self." [3] Humility isn't putting ourselves down, but rather lifting others up. It puts others first, thinking of their needs, ideas, and desires before our own (Philippians 2:3-4).

WHO WANTS TO BE HUMBLED?

We might try our best to be humble. However, we aren't eager to jump into situations that would humble us. In fact, we avoid them if we can. Though people might strive to be humble, would anyone ever choose to be humbled?

Jesus did. He actually made the decision to be humbled. In fact, He made Himself nothing and laid aside His privileges in heaven because He loved us so much. He "humbled himself by becoming obedient to the point of death, even death on a cross" (Philippians 2:8).

Our pride still gets in the way at times, but in spite of our sin, Jesus continues to offer us grace. The Apostle Peter knew this all too well. Several times the Lord had to put Peter's pride to task, even once telling His impetuous disciple, "Get behind Me, Satan!" (Matthew 16:23). Later a humbler Peter would write, "God is opposed to the proud, but gives grace to the humble. Therefore humble yourselves under the mighty hand of God, that He may exalt you at the proper time, casting all your anxiety on Him, because He cares for you" (1 Peter 5:5-7). If we humble ourselves, we don't have to worry about who will take care of us. We won't be forgotten. God will watch over us (Psalm 121).

So what does humility look like in our daily lives? Perhaps these ideas can help us better walk humbly with our God, one step at a time (Micah 6:8).

Be ready to admit your faults (James 5:16). Take feedback and criticism graciously by acknowledging, "Thanks for letting me know" (Proverbs 27:17). Pray to see any kernel of truth that might be there and let go of the rest. An unknown author quipped, "Swallow your pride occasionally, it's non-fattening!" [4]

Use every opportunity to help others succeed. Share any knowledge that might help them. Be open to learn from others and acknowledge them when they help you. Praise them when they do well. Encourage them when they mess up (1 Thessalonians 5:11).

Don't talk about yourself so much. Let others praise you (Proverbs 27:2). When you do a good deed, don't dwell on it (Matthew 6:2-4). An old proverb states, "Spoil not an act of kindness by speaking of it" [5] Give God all the glory.

If you are forgotten or slighted, don't take offense. Either it was done accidentally or on purpose. If someone slighted you unintentionally, she would be embarrassed to know her mistake. If done on purpose, take the higher road, and move on. Think of Jesus who was maligned and forsaken (Matthew 27:46).

Be willing to serve others however you can. Look for opportunities to go last in line, help with a package, and run an errand for others, even when it is not convenient. Jesus came to serve; so should we. When Jesus washed the disciples' feet, He demonstrated that it took a strong self-image to truly serve humbly (John 13:3-5). We can feel strong and secure in God's love for us. As author G.K. Chesterton observed, "It is always the secure who are humble." [6]

GOING FURTHER

1. How might have Naaman suffered physically, socially, and emotionally from his disease?
2. What godly qualities of the Israelite servant girl demonstrated her faith in God and Elisha, even though she had been taken from her home?
3. Why do you think Naaman felt insulted by Elisha sending Gehazi to tell the officer to dip in the Jordan River seven times? How did the expectations of his rank and position clash with Elisha's humility?
4. How would you describe the dramatic "before/after" transformation in Naaman's body and soul after he did what Elisha asked?
5. Why do you think Elisha remained detached from Naaman's healing? Why did Naaman want to take home some dirt from Israel?
6. How did Elisha's attitude about receiving gifts differ from Gehazi's attitude? What were some possible motives for Gehazi's greed?
7. How does our humility depend on an understanding of who God is and our relationship with Him?

8. Who were some humble women in the Bible? How did they demonstrate in difficult situations that they found their confidence and security in the Lord?

9. How was Jesus humble in everyday ways? How far did He go to humble Himself?

10. What are some ways we can learn to better walk humbly with our God?

WHO ELSE?

Who else returned to his healer to thank Him (Luke 17:15)?

A LEAP OF FAITH: WORKING FOR HAPPIER FAMILIES

Growing up in a happy home compelled Beth Wilson to make her life's work helping others enjoy such a blessing. For her, majoring in family and consumer sciences in college was a natural choice. After obtaining her doctorate, she taught those courses at Harding University for over 40 years.

Disturbed by domestic violence in her community, Beth took a leap of faith and volunteered for a local shelter for abused women. Statistics show that 33% of women worldwide will be abused in their lifetime. In the abusive homes in America, children are 60% more likely to be abused and grow up to abuse others or marry abusers. Homelessness caused by domestic violence is on the rise.

Even with her training, Beth was unsure how she could help others in these situations. After more than two decades of volunteer work with the shelter, she has learned much. She has led the weekly support group and realizes that this kind of violence can happen to any man, woman, or child.

She had to learn to love the abusers as God loves them, especially those who use the Bible to justify their abuse. When she received negative comments about her work, she had to clarify her purpose: to keep women and children from harm, offering them love and acceptance and helping them explore their options. Now in retirement, Beth continues to help women know the true meaning of love because some of them have been abused by someone every day of their lives.

Beth has received more than she's given, saying, "True happiness comes from serving others." [7] When she receives sticky hugs from children freed from abuse, she thanks God for opportunities to bring some happiness into their lives.

CHAPTER 9

OPENING YOUR EYES

2 Kings 6:8-23

The world of spies and espionage has always been intriguing. In popular books and movies, secret agents showcase the latest technological gadgets to defy overwhelming odds and uncover classified information. If they are fortunate enough to obtain such critical intelligence, these agents can save the lives of their citizens and protect their homeland by outsmarting the enemy.

In the Bible, the first mention of spying goes all the way back to Genesis. Joseph accused his brothers of spying to find any weak areas in Egypt's defense, but he was acting under a ruse himself (Genesis 42:9). He later "blew his cover" when he revealed his identity as their brother. Spying must have been an established fact of life in Egypt, well-known to Joseph.

Years later, Moses commissioned 12 spies for an intelligence operation to check out the Promised Land. When they returned, they brought back news of a land "flowing with milk and honey" (Exodus 3:8). Ten of the spies, however, reported that they could not conquer the land because the powerful Canaanites made them seem like grasshoppers. Joshua and Caleb urged them to take the land, and they were almost stoned by the mob. Because they trusted in God, Joshua and Caleb were allowed to enter the Promised Land. For the peoples' lack of faith, all those older than 20 years were prevented from entering the land and were destined to wander for 40 years in the wilderness (Numbers 13-14).

Forty years later Joshua sent a smaller covert operation of two spies to Jericho to spy out the city. They ended up in Rahab's house, perhaps because newcomers to a city might be expected to visit an innkeeper or a harlot without being questioned. Instead of reporting them to the king of Jericho, Rahab hid the spies and rerouted those searching for them. Her "espionage" not only saved the spies, but also the lives of her and her family (Joshua 2).

These are not all the spy operations in the Bible, but they give us an idea how spies worked at that time. However, none of the spies fit the profile of the informant, Elisha. Most spies before him had to search for their information. But God gave the information directly to Elisha to use against their enemy, Aram.

SPEAKING THEIR LANGUAGE

At this time, Elisha's intelligence reports were extremely valuable to Israel. The relative peace between Aram and Israel when Naaman was healed didn't last forever. The nations were at war, but "war" at this point meant border skirmishes and not a full-scaled conflict (2 Kings 6:8, 23). However, Aram was the superior power. It was evident the Arameans had the upper hand when they could easily march to Dothan within about 10 miles of the capital Samaria without interference from Israel's army.

The Arameans formed a loose confederation of settlements and towns in the area of what is now Syria, with Damascus as their capital. When they were threatened, they were quick to ally with other countries or each other. When each crisis was over, they disbanded and often ended up fighting each other or their former allies. Around the beginning of Israel's monarchy, they became a powerful political force, but King David later defeated them and demanded tribute from them (2 Samuel 8:5-6).

What bound the Arameans together more than their politics was their language. Similar to Hebrew, the Aramaic language eventually replaced it as the official international language. In the Old Testament, parts of Ezra, Daniel, and Jeremiah were written in Aramaic. By New Testament times, Aramaic seemed to be the language of the Jewish common people while Hebrew remained the language of the Jewish upper class, as well as for religious and governmental functions. Even though the Arameans were not a long-lasting political force, their contribution of the Aramaic language was an important one, as it was spoken from Egypt to Persia and was influential in writing the Bible.

THE SECRET AGENT WHO WASN'T A SECRET

Agent Elisha's modus operandi was simple. When the king of Aram planned an ambush on Israel, Elisha would warn the king of Israel to be on his guard at each location. In those days, prophets commonly gave military advice to kings. Elisha's information was always correct, worthy only of a top agent sent from God (2 Kings 6:8-10). This frustrated and enraged the king of Aram.

However, Elisha's identity as an informant was eventually discovered. One of the Aramean king's servants knew that the informant who knew the position of their troops wasn't a traitor to the king but was Elisha himself. Somehow, someone found out that it was the prophet who knew the very words the king spoke in his bedroom (2 Kings 6:12). Elisha was the "fly on the wall" informant.

The king of Aram saw Elisha as a threat and ordered his soldiers to find and capture him. Ironically, they didn't initially know where he was, but Elisha knew where the army of Aram was, with the Lord's help. They eventually reported back that he was in Dothan. So the king tried to solve his problem of troop movements by moving more troops!

The king sent his large army with horses and chariots, the most sophisticated military equipment of that time. By the size of the army commissioned for the task, the king of Aram must have thought that Elisha's capture might be difficult. They arrived by night and surrounded the city of Dothan, which was built on a hill with a view of the roads in four directions. Did the king of Aram think this horsepower could overpower the strength of God Almighty, who had already seen everything he did?

The next morning Elisha's servant saw that they were surrounded by the Aramean army and exclaimed, "'Alas, my master! What shall we do?' So he [Elisha] answered, 'Do not fear, for those who are with us are more than those who are with them'" (2 Kings 6:16). At first Elisha's servant could not understand, but then the prophet prayed that the Lord would open his eyes so that he could see. Then his servant saw the spiritual army with horses and chariots of fire around Elisha, forming a protective bodyguard for him. God's army had much more "firepower" than the Arameans.

The Aramean army came to where Elisha was, but they didn't recognize him. God could have warned Elisha to escape, but instead He led the army right to him. Then Elisha prayed, and God temporarily struck them blind. He told the blinded soldiers truthfully that he would lead them to the man they sought. Whether Elisha meant himself or the king of Israel, he led them to his hometown Samaria (2 Kings 6:32). He didn't pretend to be anyone different than who he was. He didn't have to pretend. He had an angelic army guarding him.[1]

TRAPPED IN SAMARIA

The trip of about 10 miles from Dothan to Samaria took a while, since Elisha was leading blinded men to the Israelite capital. When they arrived, Elisha prayed again for their eyes to be opened. They discovered they were trapped inside Israel's capital. Instead of entrapping Elisha, he had trapped them.

The king of Israel asked Elisha if he should kill the captives. Elisha took a leap of faith and gave an amazing answer: Don't kill them, but provide a meal for them! The prophet asked the king if he would kill soldiers he had captured. Captives taken as plunder were at the mercy of the victor, who could sell them, enslave them, or set them free.

Perhaps the king of Israel wanted to avoid repeating his father Ahab's mistake when he had previously let Aram's king go free (1 Kings 20:42). Possibly that was the case, but this time the circumstances were different from his father's situation. Elisha reasoned that the king of Israel would not routinely slaughter soldiers who had walked into Samaria without a fight. Instead Elisha commanded they be fed a meal and sent back home.

Why didn't God authorize the destruction of the Arameans? They had been a thorn in Israel's side by attacks ranging from border clashes to full-scale war. At times in Israel's history, God had commanded that all living things and possessions be dedicated to Him by totally destroying them. (The exceptions of gold, silver, or iron, which couldn't burn, were designated for the tabernacle or temple.) This principle of *herem* referred only to the nation of Canaan and the Amalekites (Deuteronomy 20:16-18; 1 Samuel 15:2-3).

Israel was to treat all other nations outside of Canaan differently (Deuteronomy 20:10-15). Even when God authorized His people to march against other nations, He did not give them the right to treat them brutally and abuse their dignity and human rights. In this particular instance, the Arameans were offered terms of peace. [2]

Elisha literally prepared a table in the presence of his enemies (Psalm 23:5). The prophet fostered friendly relationships between Israel and Aram by setting them free and providing a sumptuous feast for them. The Arameans saw a dramatic demonstration of God's grace. What a way for Israel to win the war—by feeding them, not defeating them! The meal served to seal forgiveness and friendship. One who had "broken bread" with another was bound not to kill him. The result was that Aram temporarily stopped their raids on Israel (2 Kings 6:23).

The Arameans were not captured by the king of Israel's military prowess, but by the hand of God. Israel's God was too powerful for them. The Lord wanted both kings and their armies to realize that the national security of Israel was dependent on God Almighty. Aram's great army with its mighty horses and chariots did not frighten Elisha. He had no reason to fear because God let Elisha see His horses and chariots of fire!

SEEING BEYOND OUR EYES

Did you notice how often sight or lack of it played a pivotal role in this incident from Elisha's life? God made a vivid impression of His nature on the Arameans by His capability to take away and restore sight. They recognized how futile it was to oppose the omnipotent God of Israel. It took the Arameans losing their sight to truly see God's power.

SIGHT	"BLINDNESS"
God helps Elisha "see" Aramean troop movements to warn the king of Israel (2 Kings 6:8-10).	Aramean king can't see how Israel knows Aram's troop movements and accuses his officers of disloyalty (6:11).
Elisha's servant sees the great Aramean army circling the city and asks the prophet what to do (6:15).	Servant can't see hills full of God's army of horses and chariots of fire all around Elisha (6:15).
Elisha prays, and his servant sees the heavenly host (6:16-17).	Elisha prays, and the Arameans are blinded and led to Samaria (6:18-19).
Elisha prays, and God opens their eyes when trapped in Samaria (6:20).	

Today, how often have we been blinded by our fear, "busy-ness," or pride to see God's power in our lives or the lives of others? We can be so plagued by worry that we minimize what God can do in our lives. We miss the times when He does something incredible because we are too busy to notice, or we rely on our own strength. We are like Elisha's servant. All we see is our enemy Satan approaching, and we wonder, *What shall we do?* We don't have the spiritual vision to see the Lord Almighty, ready to protect and defend us.

INCREASING OUR AWARENESS

It is difficult for us as humans to fathom how mighty our God is. We think in much smaller terms. This "spiritual downsizing" limits God's power in our minds. Instead, we need to "magnify" our view of God and remember how awesome and powerful He actually is. We need to be alert to the many things He does and give Him glory. Just think how the power of prayer and God's love have changed countless lives. People complain how devastating "acts of God" can be, but they forget they receive many blessings from God on a daily basis. The beauty of the seasons, the magnificence of mountains and oceans, and the wonder of creation are amazing displays of His majesty (Romans 1:20).

Just like Elisha prayed for his servant, we need to pray that God will enable us to see things in a spiritual light. That's also what Paul prayed for the Ephesians. In his prayer, it seems Paul actually made up a fascinating term, "the eyes of your heart," with "heart" referring to their spiritual and intellectual life.[3]

Paul wrote, "I pray that the eyes of your heart may be enlightened" (Ephesians 1:18). In verse 19, he stressed four words (*power, working, strength,* and *might*) with similar meanings to underscore the majesty and scope of God's power. That same power raised Jesus from the dead and exalted Him in heaven. That power worked through God's people like Elijah and Elisha, and it can also work through us.

Paul knew God's strength personally in his life. "For this purpose also I labor, striving according to His power, which mightily works within me" (Colossians 1:29). He believed that understanding the power of God would help Christians in their daily spiritual walk, so he prayed that they might have a deeper grasp of that power. He emphasized how the incomparable power of God in and through believers makes incredible things possible.

IMPROVING OUR SPIRITUAL VISION

How can we improve our spiritual vision to realize God's power? We can start by cultivating more of an eternal mindset each day.

Focus not on what is seen, but what is not seen (2 Corinthians 4:18). Remember "we walk by faith, not by sight." Our citizenship is in heaven, where God's power will transform us (2 Corinthians 5:7; Philippians 3:20-21).

However, we can't have spiritual 20/20 vision if we are ignoring what is going on around us. Keeping up with current events can help us be ready to help people who need it. Instead of bemoaning the sad state of world events, we can pray about what is happening, believing in God's power to work in men's affairs. "First of all, then, I urge that entreaties and prayers, petitions and thanksgivings, be made on behalf of all men, for kings and all who are in authority, so that we may lead a tranquil and quiet life in all godliness and dignity" (1 Timothy 2:1-2).

We also need to open our eyes to everyday opportunities to grow. Be intentional about studying and understanding God's Word: "Open my eyes, that I may behold wonderful things from Your law" (Psalm 119:18). We should do what it takes to carve out time in our busy schedules to focus on Scripture. The Word of God has the power to change our lives (Hebrews 4:12).

We can show God's love in good deeds. In the workplace, at ballgames, and on the highway, treat people in a way that mirrors Christ. Look beyond the person you see to truly see the person within. Pray that the eyes of her heart will be opened to see God's power working in you and others. Perhaps her eyes will be opened, and she will see a reflection of Christ living in you!

GOING FURTHER

1. How was Elisha's intelligence operation with the Aramean troops different from other examples of spying in the Old Testament? ?

2. What lasting legacy did the Arameans leave of their culture? What part did the Aramaic language play in the writing of the Bible?

3. How did Dothan's location make viewing the soldiers circling the city possible for Elisha's servant? How did he react when he saw the army?

4. How did God's power in giving and taking sight play a role in Elisha's dealings with the Arameans?

5. What was incredible about Elisha's treatment of the Aramean soldiers? How did God show His power and grace through Elisha?

6. Why didn't God authorize the wholescale destruction of the Arameans?

7. How can our perception of God affect our prayer life? How can we "spiritually downsize" God in our minds?

8. How can our limited spiritual vision cause us to react like Elisha's servant in the face of trouble?

9. How does it make you feel to know that the power that enabled Jesus to rise from the grave is the power that can work in us?

10. How can we have an eternal mindset while still being open to the needs of others in our everyday lives? What are some other specific ways to improve our spiritual vision?

WHO ELSE?

Who else's eyes were opened to see someone's true identity (Luke 24:13-27)?

A LEAP OF FAITH: TAKING ON LIFE WITH AN UNBREAKABLE SPIRIT

If you've ever seen Kid President Robby Novak on YouTube, you can imagine how proud his parents Laurie and David Novak are. They adopted Robby and his sister, Lexi, and the Novak household hasn't been the same since.

Their story together began when the Novaks took a leap of faith to become foster parents. They didn't go into foster parenting to adopt, but to give children a temporary home until they found a permanent one. After raising two biological children with one teenager at home, they decided to take in 12 foster children over a period of seven years. When they considered adopting Lexi and Robby, their biological children gave their wholehearted approval and love.

At first Laurie didn't know much about Osteogenesis Imperfecta (OI), the condition that Robby and Lexi have. She learned quickly about this genetic condition known for fragile, brittle bones that currently has no known cure. Trips to the emergency room for broken bones became a common occurrence.[4] The Novaks decided to allow the children to participate in as many physical activities as possible, letting them answer, "Is it worth a break?" for risky ones. They want their children to experience a full life. Experts agree that though it may seem activity should be discouraged, exercise can actually help build strong muscles that protect weak bones. So Laurie believes in letting her kids be kids. She says, "They have to be loved for how they are and treated as normal as possible." [5]

Laurie says about their life: "If we can do it, anyone can. God's dreams are bigger than our dreams. We never could have imagined how much adoption would change our lives and how much we would be blessed by it." [6]

REPORTING GOOD NEWS

2 Kings 6:24-7:20

Have you ever wondered why there seems to be so much bad news reported these days? Some people blame it on politics, while others point to the extensive coverage of worldwide disasters and conflicts. Also to blame is the invasive nature of news itself, which lays bare the private lives of people, displaying their faults for all to see. No wonder good news is so refreshing. As one song put it, "We sure could use a little good news today." [1]

The job of an Old Testament prophet was much like a modern news reporter. Elisha was God's reporter "on the ground," and he just told it like it was, complete with late-breaking news and live updates on location. He had to differentiate between fake and real news. Reporting the news, whether it was good or bad, just came with his job.

GOOD AND BAD NEWS FROM ARAM

The good news was that after Elisha's gracious treatment of Aramean soldiers, Aram suspended its intermittent attacks on Israel along the border for a time (2 Kings 6:23). This temporary lull could have given Israel time to reflect on God's compassion and love and eventually come back to Him. The bad news was that during those years, Israel did not repent. So some time later, God allowed Ben-Hadad, Aram's king, to invade Israel all the way to Israel's capital, Samaria. Scholars are not certain which Ben-Hadad this was. (Some scholars believe there were at least three Ben-Hadads!)

Samaria was under siege, which prevented all trade and business from leaving or entering. Food became scarce. The people suffered from extreme hunger. They grew desperate. The military purpose of a siege was to drive the citizens of the city to such dire starvation and thirst that they would surrender without a fight. So it became a contest of wills to see who could last the longest—the people inside or the army outside.

Samaria's lengthy siege led to a famine, which, in turn, produced exorbitant prices for the least edible food, *if* it was available. The average wage at that time was about a shekel per month. That gives some perspective on how much was charged for undesirable things to eat. A donkey's head cost 80 shekels and dove's dung or thorny acacia pods cost five shekels (2 Kings 6:25).[2]

A LAST RESORT

Cannibalism could be a last resort in such dire times. Because of Israel's disobedience, God's prophets foresaw the extremity of starvation that could prompt cannibalism (Deuteronomy 28:56-57). One day the Israelite king stumbled on such a case. As he walked along the wall one day surveying Samaria, a woman cried out for help. The king answered that if the Lord didn't help her, where could he, as the king, get help? She then explained about the decision that she and another mother had made. Thinking that they were going to starve, they agreed to eat their children. This woman had cooked her son one day for them to eat, but the next day the other mother had hidden her son.

On hearing such news from the woman, the king was so distraught that he did not even deal with the horrific plan of both mothers or the deception of the one who hid her son. Such a calamity horrifies us as it did the Israelite king that day. Probably in an expression of anger toward God and Elisha, he tore his robe, revealed the sackcloth he wore underneath, and vowed to have Elisha killed.

OFF WITH ELISHA'S HEAD!

Although sackcloth was usually worn as a sign of repentance or mourning, the king of Israel did not demonstrate these feelings when he threatened to cut off Elisha's head. Why did he blame Elisha for the calamity on Israel enough to demand his death? Did the king think that removing Elisha from the picture would solve his problem? Perhaps Elisha had previously advised him to withstand the siege with the promise of deliverance. When rescue seemed inconceivable, it is possible the king felt betrayed by the prophet, abandoned by God, and ready to find a scapegoat for a seemingly impossible situation.

However, the king had failed to put the blame where it truly belonged. He had forgotten that it was his sins and the sins of the people of Israel that had put them in this predicament. Centuries before, Moses had foretold the blessings and cursings of God's covenant. If God's people obeyed His law, they would be bountifully blessed, but if they disregarded His law, they would be cursed (Deuteronomy 28-30). Cannibalism was specifically described in Deuteronomy 28:53: "Then you shall eat the offspring of your own body, the flesh of your sons and of your daughters whom the Lord has given you, during the siege and the distress by which your enemy will oppress you."

The king sent a messenger to Elisha's house to kill him, but the prophet was not taken off guard. God had given Elisha foreknowledge of this threat as he sat with the elders in his house. These elders represented leading families in the tribe or town, and they were suffering in the siege with him. They chose to wait with the prophet of God instead of the king. No doubt they were waiting for an oracle from Elisha either to proclaim that deliverance was imminent or to recommend anything they could do about the situation.

Elisha asked the elders with him, "Do you see how this son of a murderer has sent to take away my head" (2 Kings 6:32)? He nailed the true character of the king in his description, meaning that the king came from a class of murderers (think Ahab and Jezebel). Elisha told the elders to bar the door and keep the king's hit man out because the king would be following closely behind. The king sent the messenger to tell Elisha that he blamed God for the catastrophic events of Samaria and saw no reason to wait any longer for the Almighty to save them.

BROADCASTING THE GOOD NEWS

In response to the king's lack of faith in God and His prophet, Elisha proclaimed some wonderful news: At the same time the next day, food would be available for sale at the gate of Samaria. The king's royal officer ridiculed the prophet's words, thinking them preposterous. He was skeptical that such a turnabout of events could happen overnight. Elisha again prophesied, noting that the royal officer would see the prophecy fulfilled, but not eat of it (2 Kings 7:2). His lack of faith caused him to miss out on God's blessing. Elisha was allowed to live, but the royal officer faced a different fate for his mockery of God, His messenger, and His message.

At the city gate of Samaria were four men suffering from a skin disease (2 Kings 7:3). The Law excluded people with skin diseases from living among others in the community (Leviticus 13:46; Numbers 5:2-3). These men were weighing their options to survive. They knew they wouldn't be welcome in town where food was so expensive and scarce. They also knew if they remained where they were, they would certainly die. Surrendering to the Arameans seemed a viable option because there was a chance they might be spared. If they were killed, it would most likely be a swift death instead of the slow starvation they could expect if they did nothing.

At twilight, the lepers moved quietly to the Aramean camp and saw no one. Entering a tent, they filled their starving stomachs and found silver, gold, and clothes, which they hid. Then they entered another tent and found more bounty to hide. Their big question: *Where is everybody?*

What they didn't know was that the Lord had sent a sound of a great army with horses and chariots. The Arameans thought that the king of Israel had hired Hittite and Egyptian kings to attack them. The noise so terrified the army, no doubt awakened from their sleep, that they abandoned their camp and everything in it. There had not been time to assess the situation or maybe even get dressed. Can't you see them scrambling over one another in a mass exodus, running for their lives as they took off toward home?

The four outcasts came to their senses and realized that they couldn't keep this good news to themselves. They had to let the people in Samaria know. They also feared punishment by God or man if they hoarded such blessings. So they hurried to tell the city gatekeepers, who shouted it to the people. Soon the good news was reverberating throughout Samaria where it also reached the king.

The king of Israel thought such unbelievable news too good to be true. In the night, he called his officers to him. He called the disappearance of the army a possible ruse to lure the Israelites into their enemy camp, ambush them, and take over the unprotected Samaria. Even then, the king did not believe that God was working to save the city, but instead felt the empty camp was an Aramean war strategy. One servant suggested sending five horses with men in two chariots to scout out what had really happened. So a scouting party was sent to the Aramean camp on a suicide mission to find out the truth.

When the scouts returned, they had staggering news — it was true! In their panic, the Arameans had scattered equipment and clothing all the way to the Jordan River. When the people heard the news, they took off in a mad rush to plunder the Aramean camp and in their pandemonium trampled the king's royal officer to death in the gateway of the city. Elisha's prophecies about him and the supply of food had been fulfilled.

Elisha's good news broadcast that God again had shown mercy and grace to His undeserving children. When hope was lost for the people inside Samaria and even when they didn't deserve it, God's grace saved them in a way much more than anyone could have imagined.

KEEPING THE GOOD NEWS TO OURSELVES?

If there were any unlikely candidates for bearing good news, it would be the four men at Samaria's city gate. Sick, scarred, and shunned because of their disease, these outcasts didn't have anything good to proclaim. Their future looked grim no matter what they did. What joy they must have experienced when they discovered the food and treasures in the Aramean camp!

Then they stopped to think. They began to feel a sense of injustice from keeping this "day of good news" to themselves. They no doubt remembered what it was like to be so hungry that they would walk into an enemy camp for the improbable but slight chance they would be fed. They also recognized they were accountable to their people and their king to share such an amazing turn of events. They took off at once to bear the good news.

We as Christians have some good news. Through an amazing turn of events, God offered His grace to everyone by sending His Son to take our place on a cross that we deserved. Millions are hungry for this good news, and we are accountable to take it to them. We can't keep silent. We can't keep such good news to ourselves.

But fear often holds us back. We're afraid we don't know enough to share. We might be rejected. We might look foolish. Although fear might be natural when we face something out of our comfort zone, we don't have to let it keep us silent. Even noble servants of God can be fearful at times. Paul must have seen fear in Timothy when the apostle wrote his younger son in the faith, "For God has not given us a spirit of timidity, but of power and love and discipline" (2 Timothy 1:7).

God can give us that spirit of power, love, and discipline if we earnestly seek and pray for it. It may be helpful to pray the prayer Paul prayed for the Ephesians (3:14-21), noting the specific references to power and love. If we change the pronouns to make them personal, we can pray, for example, "Now to Him who is able to do far more abundantly beyond all that *I* ask or think, according to the power that works within *me*" (Ephesians 3:20) (author's italics). God can help us overcome through His power at work in us.

To bolster your confidence, be familiar with specific Bible verses to use in bringing someone to Christ. Keep them handy in your Bible and purse. Role-play answering questions with other Christians to prepare yourself. To make it easier to understand, utilize diagrams with Scriptures to help someone visualize what obedience to the Lord involves (like a burial and resurrection in Romans 6). See if Bibles with a chain of verses would be helpful or lessons using questions to discover answers in Bible verses. A list of teaching materials like these is given in the late Stafford North's excellent book *Evangelizing Your Community* (p. 115-117).[3]

BEING A GOOD NEWS BEARER

There are several ways to share the Good News, so find the one that works for you. For example, some people prefer to have a one-on-one study or perhaps two couples together while others prefer small groups of people. Some people might prefer viewing DVDs giving a survey of the Bible. To make reaching out to others easier, one DVD series simplifies the Good News by demonstrations, examples, and Bible study.

You might feel afraid to ask someone to study with you, but many people will feel honored to be asked. If you ask politely without being pushy, you might be surprised. They might say yes. If not now, they may agree to later. If someone asks you something you don't know, just say, "I don't know, but I will try to find out." You don't have to know it all.

Online courses offer a variety of possibilities. They have the advantage of flexibility and accessibility to reach those across the country or around the world. Teachers and students can work at their own pace at their own convenience.

For example, both World Bible School (WBS) and World English Institute (WEI) teach the Bible online. (These are also available through snail mail.) WBS lessons are taken entirely from the Bible. WEI students sign up for free English lessons with the knowledge that the lessons are taken from the Bible.

Students must have a basic proficiency in English to enroll. In both WBS online (*www.worldbibleschool.org*) and WEI online (*www.worldenglishinstitute.net/*) the teacher tries to build a friendly rapport with students. The teacher is responsible for correcting a few of the students' written answers, but the program automatically grades most of the multiple-choice answers. The time spent working with the students depends on the number of students a teacher volunteers to take and how much time she can offer to help.

What rejoicing there will be when your friend, coworker, neighbor, relative, or perhaps a student you have never personally met is baptized through any of these methods! No matter which method you choose, what an indescribable feeling you will have when you have had a part in bringing someone to the Lord. And the angels will rejoice with you!

GOING FURTHER

1. Why do you think there seems to be so much bad news today? How do you think it affects people who hear it?
2. What was the military purpose of a siege? How did it physically and economically affect the people who were trapped?
3. What plan of survival did the king of Israel discover as he walked along the wall of Samaria? What was his reaction to his discovery?
4. Why was the nation of Israel to blame for Samaria's predicament? What prophecy foretold this?
5. Why did Elisha's good news seem so preposterous? What happened to the king's royal officer to fulfill Elisha's prophecy?
6. Why did the four men find the Aramean camp empty? How did the king confirm their report and what was the result?

7. How are we spiritually like the men who discovered food and treasures in the camp while their people were starving?

8. Why do you think fear keeps us from sharing the Good News? How can we overcome our fears?

9. What are some ways to share the Good News with others? What ways have you used or prefer to use?

10. If you are a Christian, who brought you to Christ? How did he/she/they teach you the Good News?

WHO ELSE?

Who else could not keep some good news to themselves (Luke 24:9-10)?

A LEAP OF FAITH: SOWING AND REAPING BEHIND BARS

No wonder Jo Anne North's late husband Stafford joked that she has done more "jail time" than a lot of criminals. For over 30 years, many women in jails and prisons have been converted because she cared enough to go and teach.

Teaching prisoners was not always on Jo Anne's radar. Two Christian male inmates inspired her to teach women in the prisons and jails around her city. She took a leap of faith, but it wasn't always easy. When she went to inquire about the possibility of teaching women in the county prison, the sheriff told her they had a chaplain and for her to give her attention to the victims. She had to make several trips before he would consent.[4] Through prayers and persistence, many prisoners were baptized. Other volunteers joined her to become teachers. They used either Bible correspondence courses or one-to-one Bible studies, teaching prisoners through glass and using a speaker to talk.

Jo Anne continues to write her converted students and to send them cards to encourage them.[5] Here is an excerpt of a student's reply:

O Dear Sister in Christ. God is surely good indeed! Your precious card and letter surely brought tears to my eyes and such warmth and love to my spirit. It is the first and only letter that I have received since I have been here...I never thought you would remember me because I don't even hear from my own family...your letter was a ray of sunshine...This will be my first Christmas without my family and friends. I've never been without them and it makes it very hard for me. Keep me in your prayers.[6]

To Jo Anne, these women are more than inmates. They are sisters.

WEEPING WHEN OTHERS WEEP

2 Kings 8:1-15

There are few more poignant sights than a man crying. It isn't that a man *shouldn't* cry. It just isn't a common sight in our world today. We understand that when a man cries, sensitive emotions have been touched. His tears provide a healthy outlet for expressing his feelings.

The ancient Jews showed their emotions more readily than people do today. Great men of faith like Abraham, Jacob, Joseph, David, Jeremiah, and Nehemiah shed tears for many reasons. Jesus wept at the tomb of Lazarus, even while knowing that He would raise him to life. He so empathized with His dear friends Mary and Martha that He felt their pain and knew their sorrow enough to weep with them.

So we are not surprised that Elisha wept. When he foresaw the suffering that Israel would experience at the hands of a wicked enemy, he had to cry. He wept for those who would weep in the days to come.

TAKING CARE OF UNFINISHED BUSINESS

Elisha had some loose ends to tie up from his mentor, Elijah. Years before, God had charged Elijah to anoint Hazael King of Aram. It was now time for Elisha to carry out this commission that God had given Elijah earlier on Mount Horeb (1 Kings 19:15-17). Hazael needed to know of his appointment ordained by God. God was about to deliver a severe judgment through Hazael on His people Israel for their flagrant disobedience and wickedness.

To find Hazael and accomplish his task, Elisha had to make the 125-mile trip from Samaria to Damascus (2 Kings 8:7). This trip would have taken about a week on foot. Damascus served as the capital of Aram where the king Ben-Hadad and his servant, Hazael, resided (1 Kings 20). This capital was also the trade center for Mesopotamia, Egypt, and Asia Minor. With such commerce, Damascus boasted a variety of exquisite goods at the king's disposal.

When Elisha arrived, Ben-Hadad was sick. He wanted an oracle from God whether or not he would recover from his illness. He sent Hazael with a gift for Elisha (2 Kings 8:9). Imagine 40 camels laden with the finest products of Damascus arriving at Elisha's door! Much like Naaman's generous gifts before, Ben-Hadad's lavish offerings to Elisha were sent in the hopes of obtaining a positive response from the prophet's God. In the ancient world, gifts were given to pagan gods to manipulate and obligate them to give a favorable oracle. Ben-Hadad was hopeful that Elisha might be influential in making his request to God.

Why would an Aramean king want to consult a prophet of Israel? In his polytheistic society, Ben-Hadad most likely acknowledged the existence and power of Israel's God even though he did not worship Him personally. The ancient world's theology was open-ended, in which any divine power was respected and any prophet was highly esteemed. Ben-Hadad didn't want to miss an opportunity to consult Elisha, who had shown that the God of Israel could work mighty wonders like healing the army commander, Naaman.

Even though at one time the Syrian king had targeted Elisha for capture or death, Elisha was now respected as a prophet who could tell the future. In fact, he had previously known what happened in the king's bedroom (2 Kings 6:12). Surely they thought that he would know the outcome of the king's present illness. It is sadly ironic that this pagan king realized he needed to consult the prophet of Israel about his illness, while previously Ahaziah, the king of Israel, sought to consult Baal-Zebub, the god of Ekron, about his illness (2 Kings 1:2). This shows the depth of apostasy to which the nation of Israel had fallen.

A PIERCING STARE

In reply to Ben-Hadad regarding his recovery, Elisha sent word through Hazael that the king would, indeed, recover from his ailment, meaning that his current illness would not cause his death. It was not terminal. Then the prophet disclosed only to Hazael that the king would ultimately die, but did not define how. So Elisha's "final answer" to Ben-Hadad's question was an enigmatic *no* and *yes* (2 Kings 8:10).

Then Elisha stared so intently at Hazael that the kings' servant felt ashamed. The prophet's penetrating gaze confirmed that he knew Hazael was a cruel man. When the Lord enabled Elisha to envision a graphic picture of Hazael's slaughter throughout Israel, the prophet wept. He could see it all too clearly in his mind's eye as he described the eventual carnage: Hazael would burn their fortresses, kill their young men, dash their little children to pieces, and rip open their pregnant women (2 Kings 8:12).

Though these descriptions seem unusually horrific to us, they were standard procedure for warring conquerors to crush rebellion. Burning fortified cities squelched any future rallying strongholds. Executing men, children, and unborn babies wiped out any hope for a present or future army. Specifically the butchery on pregnant women made certain that no male babies would live to grow up and reclaim the conquered land. The goal of this extermination was to obliterate any possible dissent or insurrection.

It is incredible that Hazael showed no revulsion to Elisha's vivid description of atrocities. Instead, Hazael only thought of power (or rather the lack of it he felt) in being able to accomplish these feats of strength. He even dismissed himself as a "dog," denoting his inferior status. Then Elisha told him that he would become king of Aram.

Although Hazael was the king's trusted official, he was not from royal lineage. Hazael was not a legitimate successor to Ben-Hadad's throne. An Assyrian inscription later confirmed this in its designation of Hazael as a commoner or usurper by calling him the "son of a nobody." [1]

Hazael was ashamed that Elisha could see his heart, but it didn't prevent Ben-Hadad's servant from committing murder. Hazael saw his opportunity to kill the king on the day after he returned to his master. To take advantage of the king's weak condition, he soaked a thick cloth in water and smothered him by covering his face. Hazael then took over Aram as its king and eventually began his campaigns against Israel and Judah.

Elisha foresaw the disastrous future for Israel at the hands of Hazael, but he could not prevent it. Whether Hazael plotted his assassination of Ben-Hadad before Elisha's revelation or he did not fathom his own evil capabilities until afterward, he should have considered the truth that Elisha presented. Elisha's announcement served as a warning to Hazael to search his heart. Hazael had a choice to do good or evil, and he chose evil.

HAZAEL'S EVIL REIGN OF TERROR

Hazael was totally responsible for his actions, and in the future, he would cause many of God's people to weep. How did Hazael fulfill Elisha's prophecy?

Hazael besieged Ramoth Gilead — Soon after he became king, Hazael flexed his military muscles and proved he was a sinister force in battle. He invaded Israel and fought a coalition of Joram, the king of Israel, with his nephew, Ahaziah, the king of Judah. This coalition was cemented by family ties of marriage, as Ahaziah's father Jehoram married Joram's sister, Athalia, daughter of Ahab (2 Kings 8:18). Hazael's army wounded Joram in battle, so he returned to Jezreel to recover, and later, Ahaziah went to visit his uncle (2 Kings 8:28-29).

Hazael conquered Transjordan — After the Assyrian king, Shalmaneser III, abandoned further attacks on Aram, Hazael was free to focus his aggression again on Israel to build a Syrian empire. During Jehu's reign of Israel, Hazael conquered the territory east of the Jordan River in all the land of Gilead from Aroer, a town by the Arnon River, to Bashan, a fertile region in the northernmost part of Palestine east of the Sea of Galilee (2 Kings 10:32-33).

Hazael invaded Judah — Hazael extended his conquest to Gath in Philistia and headed for nearby Jerusalem. Because of Judah's unfaithfulness to God, God allowed Hazael's smaller army to claim victory over Judah's larger one. The Arameans killed all the leaders of the people and severely wounded Joash, the king of Judah (2 Chronicles 24:23-25). With defeat imminent, Joash promptly negotiated Hazael's withdrawal from Jerusalem by offering him treasures from the palace and temple (2 Kings 12:17-18).[2]

Hazael crippled Israel's Army — Jehoahaz, Jehu's successor, fared worse when Hazael reduced Israel's army to such an extent that it was compared to the dust at threshing time. At this low point in Israel, it was left with only 10 chariots, 50 horses, and 10,000 soldiers in the infantry — just enough for pageantry on state occasions. Hazael almost succeeded in eliminating Israel's military force. In such dire straits, Jehoahaz sought the Lord's favor for deliverance from Hazael. God provided a deliverer, although the name of the deliverer was not given in the text (2 Kings 13:1-7, 22-23).

Hazael's ruthlessness continued until his death — At Hazael's death, Israel was finally able to halt the Aramean aggression under Hazael's son Ben-Hadad. King Jehoash, son of Jehoahaz, finally recaptured from Ben-Hadad towns that Hazael had taken from Jehoahaz (2 Kings 13:24-25).

Through Hazael, God chastised the people of Israel because of their sins (Amos 4). But God's justice and judgment also extended to those who rose against His people. Hazael committed such atrocities in Israel that the prophet Amos later invoked God's judgment on Aram: "So I will send fire upon the house of Hazael, and it will consume the citadels of Ben-Hadad" (Amos 1:4). Then Hazael's people would be the ones weeping.

A TIME TO WEEP

William Shakespeare once observed, "To weep is to make less the depth of grief."[3] Weeping can relieve some of the burden when we are gripped by sorrow, pain, or suffering. God feels such empathy with our feelings that He intimately knows our tears. David described God caring about what was happening in his life in this way: "You have taken account of my miseries; Put my tears in Your bottle, Are they not in Your book?" (Psalm 56:8).

One day God will wipe away our tears, and there will be no more pain or sorrow (Revelation 21:4). We look forward to heaven where we will weep no more. Until then, we can comfort those who weep by weeping with them.

A TIME TO BE SILENT

Someone has said that we are to empathize so profoundly with others who are hurting that we can taste the salt in their tears. We can try to find soothing words, but sometimes words are just not enough to comfort those who are suffering the pain of loss.

We can see an extraordinary example of this kind of empathy in Job's friends. When they heard about Job's misfortune, they came to be with him. "When they looked from a distance and did not recognize him, they raised their voices and wept. And each of them tore his robe, and they threw dust over their heads toward the sky. Then they sat down on the ground with him for seven days and seven nights with no one speaking a word to him, for they saw that his pain was very great" (Job 2:12-13). These first responders got it right. Later their words hurt Job deeply, but their first actions were exemplary.

Job had lost his wealth, his family, his health, and even the support of his wife. When his friends saw his pain, they wept and spoke no words for seven days. (Some of us can't go seven minutes without talking!)

Though on the surface it seems they made their trip in vain, they truly did something powerful. They gave Job their presence and stood (or rather sat) by him for several days, ready to listen and cry with him. There is a lesson for us.

Sometimes it takes more than words to show we care. On those occasions, we don't need to say anything; we just need to be there, maybe with tears, maybe with a hug, maybe with a lasagna dinner. In the initial shock of pain, the hurting person might not hear or remember the words we speak anyway. But she will certainly remember we helped clean her house, took care of the children, or shopped for groceries. Being there might mean more than words. The wise king Solomon advised that there is "a time to be silent and a time to speak...He has made everything appropriate in its time" (Ecclesiastes 3:7, 11).

A TIME TO SPEAK

There are other times when we *do* need to say something when someone is hurting. It is important to know what to say and what *not* to say. "Like apples of gold in settings of silver Is a word spoken at the proper time" (Proverbs 25:11). For example, sometimes sharing a personal or funny story about a deceased loved one can bring comfort to the one grieving. It also provides memories from which he or she can draw strength and cherish later.

Loss of Life — Express your concern with, "I love you. I am truly sorry.

Words fail me, but I care for you. It is so hard to lose a loved one. I don't understand why this happened." Avoid insensitive comments like, "God must have wanted her/him. It's for the best. It could be worse. It's time you get on with your life." Grief doesn't have a timetable; it's individual for everyone.

Loss of Home — Say something like, "I know it must be difficult to start over. The future might seem uncertain, but I'm here for you. May I pray with you? I'm here to listen." Avoid "Let me tell you what happened to me. At least you have insurance. The worst is over. It was God's will." How do we know what will happen in the future or what God's will is in another person's life?

Loss of Health — Tell her, "Your voice seems stronger today. Tell me what is helpful and what isn't. May I go with you to the doctor? Do you need to talk? Would your kids like to come over?" Avoid, "My sister died from this same thing. How much time does the doctor give you? Didn't you notice the symptoms?" The patient does not need you to make her feel more depressed.

Loss of Job — Offer support like, "That must have been a shock. What can I do to help and when? Let's pray about this now. I'll help you brainstorm ways you can network, if you like." Avoid, "Didn't you see the layoff coming? I lost a job once. I know how you feel." We can't know *exactly* how anyone else feels.

Author Jane McWhorter told the story about some friends whose child was stillborn. She left a note on the door before they arrived home from the hospital. The mother later told her how much her note meant to them. Her heartfelt message simply stated, "I cried too." [4]

GOING FURTHER

1. What were some of the reasons some great men of faith wept?

2. What was Ben-Hadad hoping to do by sending a gift to Elisha through Hazael? How did the king's belief in pagan gods play a part in his generosity?

3. How was the ancient world's open-ended view of gods much like our postmodern world today?

4. Why do you think Elisha told Hazael that the king's current illness wouldn't cause his death, but that he would ultimately die?

5. At that time, what was the military rationale for the horrific treatment of victims of war? What was significant about Hazael's reaction to Elisha's prophecy?

6. How did Hazael murder his master? Whether Elisha's revelation served as a warning or an impetus for evil in Hazael's mind, who made the choice to do evil?

7. How did Job's friends initially provide comfort for him in his loss and pain?

8. What were some times when you have experienced the presence and help of someone who was just "there"? Have you been able to help someone in this way?

9. Has someone ever wept with you when you suffered a loss? How did it comfort you?

10. Has someone ever spoken "apples of gold" words that were appropriate in your particular loss? What were those words?

WHO ELSE?

Who else wept when He foresaw the destruction of His people by invading armies (Luke 19:40-44)?

A LEAP OF FAITH: HEALING THROUGH SHARING TEARS

In 1976 Jenny Duncan's only daughter died at nine years old. There was no support group available to her, and she didn't know how to deal with her grief. She buried her feelings in her heart and went on with her life. She put a smile on her face and acted like everything was fine.

In 2009 she was asked to help with a women's grief support group in her congregation. She took a leap of faith and reluctantly agreed. She found that as she participated, she began to uncover the unresolved grief she had buried years ago. She began to recover by listening and talking with others who were grieving.

The support group meets weekly and is open to church members and the community. By advertising the group, they have made close ties and friends with the community. Four regular members guide the discussion, but they tell those present that they are not teachers or counselors. Everyone is encouraged, but not forced, to talk, with the understanding that anything they say is confidential. All in the group are given the book *Walking With Those Who Weep* to read and comment on if they wish. This helps new members fit in more easily.

One group member's husband has Alzheimer's disease, and he is in a nursing home. She is anticipating his eventual death and knows it is coming. Her grief process has already started. She has brought a new dimension to the group.

By sharing her grief, Jenny has learned that everyone grieves differently, and all their stories help to encourage others. She observes, "I've seen God work on the hearts of many people, including myself. I've seen people find closure in dealing with their loss. They see that there is a future past their grief." [5]

CHECKING YOUR MOTIVES

2 Kings 9-10

You can tell a lot about people by how they drive. A corporate CEO might act like she owns the road. The music lover turns up his stereo, blasting his favorite rap song to prove it. Your daredevil neighbor challenges herself to see how close she can tailgate your car and put on her makeup at the same time.

Centuries ago people could tell when Jehu was coming. Jehu drove his chariot like he lived — fast and furious with the zeal of a madman. But some people debate his motives. Did his zeal go too far or did it not go far enough?

DELEGATING A SECRET MISSION

Although Elisha sometimes went undercover, this time he was sending a son of the prophets on a secret mission to anoint Israel's next king (2 Kings 9:1-3). God had chosen Jehu to replace the present king, Joram (also known as Jehoram). Years before, God directed Elijah to anoint Jehu. Now Elisha would see that it was carried out. Elisha urged the messenger to accomplish his task and then run, perhaps to avoid negative reactions from Jehu or the soldiers.

After the messenger reached Ramoth Gilead, he asked to speak to Jehu in private. After he anointed Jehu, the messenger explained the divine mission: God had chosen Jehu to inflict divine judgment on Ahab's house and avenge the blood of God's prophets whom Jezebel had murdered. Then the messenger fled.

When Jehu disclosed that he had been anointed king of Israel, the other captains offered their support. Since his coup had to be kept a secret, Jehu charged his supporters not to let anyone out of

Ramoth Gilead to tell the news in Jezreel, where the kings of Israel had a summer palace (1 Kings 21:1). Jehu had to work quickly. His first task was to get to Jezreel where Joram, Ahaziah and Jezebel were before the news of his anointing reached them.

THE PURGE BEGINS

Most of Israel's troops remained in Ramoth Gilead, ready to defend against the Aramean king, Hazael. Taking some troops with him, Jehu took off like a madman in his chariot to Jezreel to begin his purge of Ahab's house.

Deaths of Joram and Ahaziah (2 Kings 9:14-29)— In Jezreel, the king of Israel, Joram, was recovering from wounds from battle. Ahaziah, the king of Judah, who was also Joram's nephew, had come to visit him. When Joram's lookout saw the rapid approach of a portion of troops from the battle at Ramoth Gilead, it meant bad news. Either they were the enemy or Israel's troops escaping enemy pursuit. When Joram's two scouts did not return, Joram and Ahaziah unwisely went out to the troops without bodyguards to protect them.

When Joram discovered Jehu's true intent, it was too late. Jehu aimed his arrow and struck Joram in the heart. Jehu told his chariot officer Bidkar to throw Joram on the very field that belonged to Naboth the Jezreelite, fulfilling the Lord's prophecy (2 Kings 9:25-26). When Ahaziah saw what had happened, he tried to escape, but soldiers also wounded him. He died in Megiddo and was carried back to Jerusalem, where he was buried (2 Kings 9:27-28).

Death of Jezebel (2 Kings 9:30-37) — When Jehu found Jezebel, she had painted her eyes and adorned her hair. She seemed ready for Jehu, as she sat by her window in the palace. Jehu ordered the eunuchs there to throw her down, where her blood spattered the wall and the horses as they trampled her body. After Jehu had a royal meal in the palace, he ordered that Jezebel be buried. By that time, the dogs had feasted on their own meal of Jezebel's body. Only her skull, feet, and hands remained in fulfillment of Elijah's prophecy (1 Kings 21:23).

BEYOND THE SEVENTY SONS OF SAMARIA

Deaths of the 70 sons (2 Kings 10:1-10) — Jehu then had to deal with Samaria, a formidable capital fortress, a stronghold for Ahab's family and a center of the Baal cult. Jehu knew he must bluff the leaders into thinking that they must fight him in battle. He wrote a letter to Samaria's leaders and Jezreel's rulers, stating that with their weapons to fight, they must choose the best heir to be king to battle for the throne. They reasoned that if two kings could not stand up to Jehu, how could they? They replied that they would do whatever he said.

Jehu's second letter to the leaders at Samaria was purposely shrewd and ambiguous. He commanded them to bring the heads of their master's sons to him. The "heads of your master's sons" could mean the high officials, like "heads of state," or their literal physical heads. The leaders promptly slaughtered the 70 princes and sent their decapitated heads to Jezreel. They were heaped in two piles at the city gate to serve as a gruesome reminder not to mess with Jehu!

Deaths of Ahab's chief men, close friends and priests (2 Kings 10:11) — The next morning, Jehu appeared before the people in Jezreel and told them that they were innocent and that he had killed the kings. Then he demanded, "… but who killed all these?" (2 Kings 10:9). Denying his responsibility for the princes' deaths, he then blamed the city leaders. He claimed a divine sanction not only for what he had done, but what he was going to do (1 Kings 21:20-24, 29). He then killed everyone there left in Ahab's house: chief men, close friends, and priests.

Deaths of Ahaziah's 42 relatives (2 Kings 10:12-14) — Jehu next set out for Samaria. Along the way, he ordered the 42 relatives of Ahaziah to be killed.

Deaths of the rest of Ahab's family (2 Kings 10:15-17) — On the road, Jehu met Jehonadab, the son of Recab. Jehu invited him into his chariot to see his zeal for the Lord. In Samaria, Jehu killed anyone left in Ahab's family.

Deaths of Baal's prophets (2 Kings 10:18-28) — Jehu planed a ruse to destroy the prophets of Baal. He set the stage for a great sacrifice to Baal and invited all the prophets from all over Israel, on penalty of death for non-attendance. With the temple crowded with Baal's prophets wearing special robes for the assembly, Jehu alerted the guards before he offered the sacrifices.

Jehu then ordered the 80 guards plus the officers outside to kill the prophets. They threw the bodies outside and then proceeded to destroy the images of Baal and tore down the temple. Jehu repurposed the temple "holy" site into a latrine, which would always remain desecrated. Jehu had essentially eradicated Baal worship in Israel for a time.

DID JEHU GO TOO FAR?

God had given Jehu a divine commission: to destroy the wicked house of Ahab and avenge the blood of God's prophets that Jezebel had shed (2 Kings 9:6-10). For fulfilling his mission, God commended Jehu (2 Kings 10:30). But what about Jehu's motives? After all, God cares not only about what His people do, but how and why they do it.

Was Jehu so filled with righteous indignation against Ahab's dynasty and its Baalism that he sincerely sought to be the Lord's instrument of judgment? Ahaziah and his relatives were of Ahab's bloodline, which gave Jehu rationale for their death sentence (2 Kings 9:27-29). Elimination of ruling families ensured that no heir felt honor-bound to avenge the previous king's death. Also some think the term "house of Ahab" extended to political supporters and government officials.[1]

However, did Jehu go too far in his purge? Where did divine sanction end and political self-interest begin? Did Jehu use God's judgment on Ahab's house to benefit his campaign to take the throne for himself? In his zeal and fury, did Jehu savagely kill more people than God approved?

The prophet Hosea recalls the massacre at Jezreel, where Jehu killed several of Judah's royal family (2 Kings 9:27; 10:11, 13-14). In Hosea 1:4, he foretold God's judgment: "I will punish the house of Jehu for the bloodshed of Jezreel, and I will put an end to the kingdom of the house of Israel."

Why would Jehu's God-ordained mission to clean up Ahab's house later be cause for punishment in Hosea 1:4? Jehu's dynasty began in Jezreel. That kingship initially destroyed Baal worship, but allowed Jeroboam I's golden calves at Dan and Bethel to remain (2 Kings 10:18-31). Generations later, that same dynasty's idol worship continued in Jeroboam II's rule (2 Kings 14:24). Even with the bloodbath at Jezreel to cleanse Israel years before, little had changed spiritually for them. For such idolatrous rebellion, Israel would face judgment for the royal house in the Valley of Jezreel in the Assyrian invasion (Hosea 1:5).[2]

Although Jehu accomplished what God directed, his motives remain in question. If Jehu had truly loved God and was sincere in doing His will, he would have removed any kind of idolatry. Though God initially praised Jehu, he and his dynasty proved to be dismal failures in leading Israel back to God.

JEHU DIDN'T GO FAR ENOUGH

When Jehu completed his divine mission, God granted him security on his throne and promised that his offspring would reign on Israel's throne to the fourth generation. His dynasty lasted longer than any other dynasty in Israel. It survived nearly 100 years, including the reigns of Jehoahaz, Jehoash, Jeroboam II, and Zechariah (2 Kings 15:12).

But Jehu did not go far enough in his zeal for spiritual reform. He did not keep the law of God with all his heart (2 Kings 10:31). God sent judgment on him and his descendants for their disobedience in allowing the worship of the golden calves to continue at Bethel and Dan. Jehu and those after him had to deal with the threat of the Aramean army of Hazael or his son Ben-Hadad II for most of their reigns until Jeroboam II (2 Kings 14:25). God's judgment came on Zechariah, Jehu's great-great grandson, who was assassinated by Shallum only six months after he took the throne (2 Kings 15:10).[3] Jehu's dynasty came to a swift end, much like the fast and furious way it had begun.

THE MOTIVE IS THE KEY

Murder mystery novels are popular because they ask two basic questions that the reader is "dying" to know. The principle question is, *Who committed the murder?* But that answer often hinges on the more intriguing one: *Why did he/she/they do it?* Discovering the motive is one of the main challenges for the police. The motive is the key. If they figure out the motive, they can more easily narrow down the suspects until they catch the guilty one(s).

The true motive of Jehu's heart remains a mystery to us. His motive is key to understanding why he did what he did. As humans, we can judge his actions, but we can't know his heart. Only God knows his heart, and He will judge Jehu's actions according to His will.

The motive is the key for us, too. Why do we serve God anyway? We can serve God for years, but do it for the wrong reasons. Let's look at some wrong motives to see if any might be lurking in our hearts. Perhaps you can think of others. The Apostle Paul wrote, "Test yourselves to see if you are in the faith; examine yourselves! Or do you not recognize this about yourselves, that Jesus Christ is in you—unless indeed you fail the test?" (2 Corinthians 13:5).

- **Praise** — Do you want other people to see how good you are, so they will notice or commend you?

- **Legalism** — Do you feel like you must check off a never-ending "spiritual to-do list" of deeds to be eternally saved, but you just can't keep up?

- **Power** — Does what you do for God make you feel important and empowered so that you can tell others what to do?

- **False Guilt** — Do you feel obligated to serve God from a sense of guilt, trying to cleanse your heart by your own works?

- **Pressure** — Do you always fill the gap because "no one else will do it" and then feel bitter and imposed upon because of your burden?

Faulty motives like these not only displease God, but they also can cause our Christian walk to become complacent. They can deplete our joy. They can snuff out our enthusiasm and initiative. Eventually people will notice what is (or isn't) driving us. We will discourage and disillusion fellow Christians and damage our credibility among those we serve.

The fact is that faulty motives can't shame, legislate, or intimidate us toward spiritual maturity. Only worthy motives can inspire us to be faithful throughout a lifetime of godly service. We just have to find the right ones.

FINDING THE RIGHT MOTIVE

Probably the hardest person to scrutinize your personal motives is the person you see in the mirror. We can be like King David, who easily saw the crime of the rich man who stole the poor man's pet lamb. Yet his vision was clouded when it came to his own crimes of adultery with Bathsheba and murder of her husband, Uriah (2 Samuel 12:1-14). In Psalm 139, David sought God's total inspection of his motives: "Search me, God, and know my heart; Put me to the test and know my anxious thoughts; And see if there is any hurtful way in me, And lead me in the everlasting way" (23-24).

Paul often wrote of his motivation for serving God (Philippians 1:21). He endured incredible suffering for the cause of Christ, but he realized that without the right motives, even his suffering would be futile. He capsulated the motivation that all Christians should have in 1 Corinthians 13:1-7. Paul makes the point that we can do all kinds of noble and sacrificial acts of service — exemplifying a faith that moves mountains, giving all our possessions to the poor, and even surrendering our bodies to be burned. Yet if we don't have love for God and others as our motivation, it doesn't matter one bit. It would all be in vain.

Paul then gives us a description of how this motivation of our hearts is demonstrated every day. Love is fleshed out in our lives as patience, kindness, and humility. It is good-tempered and forgiving. It finds joy in the truth. It "bears all things, believes all things, hopes all things, endures all things" (1 Corinthians 13:7, ESV). So we need to ask ourselves: *Are our actions characterized by love?* This is our heart checkup. How well are we doing?

Periodically, it will help us to step back, step down, and step up to find our motivation for serving God. First, step back and think, *Why am I serving God? What drives me? What are my motives?* Then step down and ask, *How can I take myself off the throne of my heart? How can I deny myself, take up my cross, and follow Him* (Matthew 16:24)? Last, step up and envision, *How can I take on a greater challenge of godly living? How can I love my Savior and others more* (Luke 10:27)?

Checking our hearts can help us be certain our motives are pure. Let us say with David, "Let the words of my mouth and the meditation of my heart be acceptable in Your sight, O Lord, my rock and my Redeemer" (Psalm 19:14, ESV).

GOING FURTHER

1. What was Jehu's two-fold commission to accomplish? After Jehu was anointed, why did he have to act quickly and secretly to get to Jezreel where Joram, Ahaziah, and Jezebel were?

2. Why do you think Jezebel had painted her eyes and adorned her hair when Jehu arrived? What was unusual about her death?

3. How did Jehu fulfill prophecy in the deaths of Joram and Jezebel?

4. How did Jehu's letters dupe Samaria's leaders? Who died as a result?

5. What was Jehu's plan for executing the prophets of Baal and destroying Baal's temple? How did mandatory attendance for all priests and the prophets' special robes work to Jehu's advantage?

6. Why was it so spiritually detrimental for Israel when Jehu allowed the golden calves at Dan and Bethel to remain? How did this demonstrate the true spiritual condition of his heart?

7. How can wrong motives for serving God adversely affect our joy, enthusiasm, and initiative? What are some examples of how this can happen?

8. Why is it so difficult for us to view our own motives objectively?

9. What was Paul's description of what our motivation should be to serve God? How does this play out in our daily lives at home, at work, and in the church?

10. What questions can we ask to periodically give ourselves a spiritual heart checkup?

WHO ELSE?

Who else sought to exterminate a family dynasty (2 Kings 11:1-3)?

A LEAP OF FAITH: MAKING THE BIBLE FUN AFTER SCHOOL

For many children, the hours between the end of school and dinner are wasted on insipid TV shows and mind-numbing video games. Seeing the need for spiritual leadership in children's lives prompted Andy Hutchinson and her husband Brad to offer an alternative at two different congregations where they worshipped. In a leap of faith, they and other members of each congregation began a fun Wednesday after-school program that ran for several years. Around 30 children in kindergarten through sixth grade attended the program. Yet the two church total memberships each numbered about 30-40.

The 1.5-hour program was structured. Church members picked up the children at school and took them to the building where a meal was ready for them. Next, the children played outside games like soft baseball, heard a Bible lesson inside, and did a craft or learned a how-to skill they could take home.

Andy wrote the curriculum and tied character building to the Bible lessons. The children were taught books of the Bible, memory verses, Bible stories and songs, manners, and etiquette. Occasionally, they invited guests to teach them to crochet, make butter, or play marbles. On special occasions they offered treats and sang for residents at a nursing home. They participated in an end-of-year program to which parents and friends were invited. The church invited these contacts to special events later.[4] Andy feels rewarded when students, now high school graduates, call her "Grandma Andy" to this day. They reminisce about the good times they had. Who knows how much those lessons from the Bible will bless them in the years to come! [5]

LEAVING A LASTING LEGACY

2 Kings 13:10-25

Estate planners can show us how to leave a legacy with the wise stewardship of our money. But how about leaving an eternal legacy for God? In his own way, Elisha left a lasting legacy that impacted many people for good despite the spiritual disobedience around him.

Even though there is at least a 40-year period of silence concerning Elisha in Scripture, he continued to influence kings, even in his last days. He faithfully served during the reigns of Ahaziah, Joram (or Jehoram), Jehu, Jehoahaz, and Jehoash (or Joash). His ministry lasted about 50 years, ranging from approximately 850-800 B.C. Taking into account his mentor/mentee relationship with Elijah, Elisha might have lived to be more than 80 years old! [1]

SHOOTING TO WIN

Toward the end of Elisha's life, kings still sought his counsel. In fact, it was soon before Elisha's death that king Jehoash visited the prophet suffering from an illness. Jehoash (or Joash) wept over him and exclaimed, "My father, my father, the chariots of Israel and its horsemen!" (2 Kings 13:14). Elisha uttered the same expression referring to Elijah when he was taken up into heaven (2 Kings 2:12). In this instance, however, Jehoash's praise for Elisha may have been uttered with honor, but not full of faith. Like the rulers before him, this king was evil and continued in the sins of Jeroboam, allowing idolatry of the golden calves at Dan and Bethel (2 Kings 13:10-11).

Jehoash did not want to lose his "point of contact" with God. He realized that it had been through the prophet's divine intervention that

Israel had been victorious against superior Aramean forces (1 Kings 20:1-34; 2 Kings 6:8-7:20). During his father Jehoahaz's reign, the army of Israel had been decimated by Hazael, king of Aram (2 Kings 13:7). Jehoash came to Elisha in distress and even though the prophet was dying, Elisha could offer words of comfort (2 Kings 13:14-19).

Elisha told the king to get some arrows and a bow. Then Elisha took the bow in his hands and placed his hands on Jehoash's hands. This was a symbolic gesture showing that God would bless the king in his battle with the Arameans. Elisha told him to open the east window and shoot an arrow. Facing the east window meant that Jehoash was facing the area of Transjordan, which at that time was controlled by Aram, but once had belonged to Israel. Elisha then told Jehoash that he would destroy the Arameans at Aphek. Destroying the city of Aphek would be a repeat of a sweet victory for Israel. Ahab had triumphed over Aram and Ben-Hadad in battle there about 60 years earlier.

Then Elisha told the king to take the arrows and strike the ground. Each strike counted as a victory against Aram. Elisha angrily counted Jehoash's three strikes as insufficient for completing the task at hand and told the king he should have struck the ground five or six times. Jehoash's moderate enthusiasm in striking would be matched with moderate success in the battle. He would be victorious three times over Aram, but complete victory over the Arameans would come through his son, Jeroboam II.

Why did God continue to bless His wayward people in ways like this? They still refused to honor and obey him, as evidenced by the Asherah pole that still stood in Samaria (2 Kings13:6). In spite of their apostasy, God provided a deliverer to escape the power of Aram. We are not told who the deliverer was. It could have been Elisha, an Israeli military general or king (Jehoash or Jeroboam II), or a foreign king distracting Aram aggression.[2] Many scholars think it was the Assyrian ruler Adad-nirari III, whose aggression against the Arameans of Damascus enabled Israel to break Aramean control of their territory.[3]

Whoever it was, what truly saved them was God's grace and compassion, going back through His covenant with Abraham, Isaac, and Jacob. Through that covenant, God was committed to Israel as people of a nation in a promised land. God at that time was unwilling to destroy or banish Judah and Israel from His presence, as they undoubtedly deserved (2 Kings 8:19; 13:23). For some time longer Judah and Israel were going to be treated the same way. But they would eventually pay for their sins and judgment would come to both nations (2 Kings 17:16-23; 25:21).

THE RUNAWAY CORPSE
Unlike Elijah's spectacular exit from the earth in a fiery whirlwind, it seemed Elisha left the earth simply, just like he lived. He grew old and sick, and then he died. This ordinary death in no way diminishes his life or ministry. In fact, there is an extraordinary footnote that no other prophet can claim in death.

At this time Moab was raiding Israel in the spring, the time for war in ancient cultures. One day some Israelites were burying a man. Since tombs were usually located in caves or dug in soft rock, they probably were going to place him in one of those. Suddenly, Moabite raiders on the warpath interrupted their task. In their scurry to get away, the Israelites quickly threw the man in a tomb, which happened to be Elisha's tomb.

When the man's corpse touched Elisha's bones, the man came to life and stood to his feet. What a strange but humorous sight it must have been to see if this resurrected man tried to follow those who were going to bury him! Or maybe he decided to hide out in the tomb until the coast was clear.

Why do you think this incredible miracle took place? A possible explanation is that with Elisha's death, the prophet whose name meant "God saves" was now gone. Israel was in a different era in which catastrophic judgment was not far away. Just as the Israelites threw the man's body in the tomb, so these Israelites were shortly going to be thrown into a "tomb of death" by being cast out of the Lord's presence into Assyrian captivity.

But there was hope, even in exile. Just as the man's body came to life when it touched the prophet's bones, so could contact with the prophets and their teaching of God's Word bring life to people dead in sin. This graphic picture of what Israel possibly could be served as a sign of hope in the devastation to come. Perhaps it was to show that God could bring life out of death, light in a time of darkness, and hope in the midst of mayhem and destruction. God wanted them to know that He still loved his people, and He still saved.

THE ELISHA-JESUS CONNECTION

How fitting that both the names of Elisha and Jesus mean "God saves"! They shared a connection in purpose even though they lived centuries apart. Several other amazing parallels exist between them. For example, they both:

- manifested God's spirit on Jordan's other side (2 Kings 2:15; John 1:28)

- praised the prophet before them (2 Kings 2:9-12; Matthew 11:11)

- transformed water (2 Kings 2:19-22; John 2:1-11)

- helped a widow in desperate circumstances (2 Kings 4:1-7; Luke 7:11-17)

- visited in the home of close friends (2 Kings 4:8; Luke 10:38-42)

- raised the dead (2 Kings 4:32-35; John 11:38-44)

- multiplied food for the hungry (2 Kings 4:42-44; Luke 9:10-17)

- ministered to the Gentiles (2 Kings 5:1-16; Mark 7:24-30)

- cleansed a man with a skin disease (2 Kings 5:1-16; Mark 1:40-45)

- had a covetous companion
  (2 Kings 5:20-27; John 12:4-6)

- had followers who left their homes
  (2 Kings 6:1-2; Matthew 18:22)

- defied gravity
  (2 Kings 6:6; Matthew 14:22-33)

- gave sight to blind
  (2 Kings 6:20; Mark 8:22-25)

- ate with sinners
  (2 Kings 6:21-23; Matthew 9:10-13)

- wept over the nation's fate
  (2 Kings 8:10-12; Luke 19:41-44)

- provided life through his death
  (2 Kings 13:20-21; 1 Peter 3:18)[4]

Although similarities exist in the lives of Elisha and Jesus, there are significant contrasts between the two. Like Elisha when he died, Jesus was put in a tomb from which people later fled. But Elisha's body would remain in the tomb and eventually decompose. Jesus' body never saw decay (Acts 2:27). In fact, Jesus rose from the grave in a resurrected body after three days, never to die again! Elisha begged God to raise the dead. Jesus demonstrated dominion over death when He raised people from the dead by commanding them to be raised.

Jesus and Elisha both performed many miracles. In fact, the Bible records Elisha performing more miracles than anyone else except the Lord. Why were so many miracles performed during these times in history? Though these miracles served to authenticate the authority of both Elisha and Jesus, they also served to call a sinful people back to God. As Jesus quoted the prophet Isaiah:

For the heart of this people has become dull,

With their ears they scarcely hear,

And they have closed their eyes,

Otherwise they would see with their eyes,

Hear with their ears,

And understand with their heart, and return,

And I would heal them (Matthew 13:15).

Truly Elisha left a lasting legacy throughout the latter half of the ninth century B.C. He proved to be an able statesman who appointed kings and a godly prophet who performed inspiring miracles. Elisha was also sensitive enough to weep over Israel's destiny. He demonstrated the power of God by overcoming impossible odds through leaps of faith. He was truly an extraordinary prophet for his times, offering grace to a people who needed to know again and again who God really was.

PASSING ON A FAITH-FILLED HERITAGE

The legacy of Elisha's extraordinary life didn't end with the sons of the prophets who appreciated his wisdom, the families who cherished his friendship, or the kings who sought his counsel. His legacy continues with us today thousands of years later as we study his life and learn from his example.

The question is, What will *your* legacy be when your life is over? Who will your life touch? What kind of a difference will your time on earth make? Although achievements in the workplace, community, and nation are definitely important and commendable, your legacy as a Christian goes far beyond that. What kind of priceless inheritance will you leave to those closest to you, your family? How will that legacy keep giving to the generations after you?

Such an inheritance is not confined to one time or place, but imparted over a lifetime of godly living. The patterns our children and other young ones in our sphere see in us during their lives will be imprinted on their souls for years to come. Where did we put our priorities? How did we model Jesus for them? Did we put God and His kingdom first (Matthew 6:33)?

If we sincerely try to follow the Lord, they will see that our faith is authentic, even when life gets difficult. If they see us holding on to an unshakable faith in shaky times, it can buoy their faith when they need courage in trying circumstances. If we have a warm, personal relationship with the Father, they will see Him as a personal God who can be loved and respected. If we teach them and incorporate spiritual principles into our daily lives, God's words will become real in their hearts (Deuteronomy 6:4-9).

Today, children face a difficult challenge to remain faithful to God in a culture where they encounter materialism, sexual temptation, and negative peer pressure. How can we prepare them to face these obstacles and live godly lives? We have a responsibility to do what we can to teach and encourage them. Even though we can't fully isolate them, we can insulate them against evil through God's Word. Like Timothy's mother, Eunice, and grandmother, Lois, we can take steps to pass on a sincere faith to our children, grandchildren, and other young ones whose lives we touch (2 Timothy 1:5).

TAKING STEPS TO PASS ON OUR FAITH

Life is too short. We must plan to make opportunities to share our faith with the younger ones we know. When we read them stories, be sure to include Bible stories. With the colorful, imaginative books and DVDs available, children can be fascinated by the exploits of Bible heroes. The Bible is exciting. Find ways to make it relevant in their daily lives. Giving them Bibles with their names engraved on them makes them feel special. Children should see us reading our Bibles so they know that Scripture is important to us.

They should also see and hear us praying for them and others. What better way to teach them how to pray than to let them pray with us? As they get older, ask them each week or month if they have some prayer requests. This helps us know what is on their hearts. Share your requests with them. If you don't live close to them, share these by phone, email, or text.

Developing family traditions can be a meaningful way to pass valuable spiritual concepts down to the next generation. Schedule a time for the family to talk about the Bible. If it is hard to set the same time every week because of everyone's activities, be flexible. Make it a fun time to bond together as a family. Be innovative in your approach. Other family traditions could include singing hymns, memorizing Scriptures, dramatizing Bible stories, volunteering for a mission trip, and setting spiritual family goals for the New Year.

Find ways to share your spiritual heritage in tangible keepsakes. For example, write down your family's story. Put it in a special memory book or scrapbook with photos. Weave God's faithfulness into the fabric of the narrative. Include specific instances showing how God has cared for your family.

Consider creating an ethical will. Its purpose is to leave those left behind with a parting message, like Jesus did in John 14-16. It often expresses love to family members as well as other topics like blessings, values, and future dreams. It can take any form and is usually shared while the writer is still living.

Keep a journal to record some of the valuable lessons you have learned in life. Your journal can be a record of your journey with God. You can include poetry, prayers, and your deepest thoughts. Should you wish, you could leave it as a personal expression of your feelings as a part of your legacy for your family when you pass away.

We all pass on a heritage to those who follow us. No matter the size of our bank account, we all pass on a spiritual legacy. With God's help, we can say with David, "The Lord is the portion of my inheritance and my cup...Indeed, my heritage is beautiful to me" (Psalm 16:5-6).

GOING FURTHER

1. In the "Hall of Faith" of Hebrews 11, what specific scenes from Hebrews 11:32-38 could point to events in Elijah's and Elisha's lives?
2. Why do you think King Jehoash sought Elisha's counsel, even when the prophet was sick and dying?
3. What were some of the symbolic gestures that Elisha used when he spoke with King Jehoash?
4. What caused the dead man's corpse to come to life? What is a possible spiritual application concerning Israel from this miracle?
5. What are some similarities in the lives of Elisha and Jesus?
6. What are some contrasts between Elisha and Jesus? What is the importance of the titles used for them like "man of God" and "Son of Man"?
7. Why is it so crucial for us as women to provide spiritual guidance to the young people who follow us? What did women in your life do to leave a spiritual legacy for you?
8. What are some specific ways that you can share your faith with the children in your life? What are some of these things that children have enjoyed with you?
9. What are some keepsakes in which you could share you spiritual heritage? Why is it priceless to show how God has worked in our lives in tangible ways?
10. How can your spiritual legacy keep giving for generations to come? What can you do this week to begin this process with a young person you know?

WHO ELSE?

Who else was connected to bones that came alive (Ezekiel 37:1-14)?

A LEAP OF FAITH: LIVING AN EXTRAORDINARY LIFE

Teacher, mentor, translator, advocate for children, amazing woman of faith—how do you describe Roberta Edwards in a few words? In 1995, Roberta and her husband took a leap of faith to plant a congregation in Port-au-Prince, Haiti. Seeing a desperate need, Roberta started taking in abandoned and orphaned children. When her native Haitian husband left five years later, they divorced.

Roberta didn't leave Haiti, but continued her work, expanding to care for 30 children in Sonlight Children's Home.[5] She taught them to take care of one another. She homeschooled them and taught them Creole, as well as French and English. She worked with them to tend a garden and raise rabbits, chickens, and tilapia for food. She instilled in them a love for God.[6]

Through the nutrition center there, she fed 160 children two meals a day, five days a week. She organized projects to help Haitians help themselves, such as teaching Haitian women to sew to support themselves and holding education workshops for Haitian teachers.

On October 10, 2015, two gunman shot and killed Roberta, 55, while she was on an errand in Haiti. Her death sent shock waves around the globe. Her life was well spent, but she will be sorely missed. Roberta has gone on to her reward. How fortunate that she left a beautiful legacy for us and so many others.[7]

Visiting teacher Rita Cochrane recalls, "If you ever mentioned to Roberta that she was something special, she would throw her head back, laugh, and say, 'No, I'm just plain ordinary Roberta.' But God... turns 'ordinary' into 'extraordinary' and that's what Robert Edwards was—*extraordinary*" (Matthew 19:26)![8]

JUMPSTARTING YOUR STUDY

The study of Elisha is full of intriguing people, places, and situations, each of which played an integral part in how God demonstrated His love for His people, even when they were disobedient to Him. Consider how the following suggestions might enhance your study. Remember to check with the Bible and reliable sources for anything you find on the Internet or in printed materials to be sure it is accurate.

Genealogies: Whether you are into your own family genealogy or not, a visual genealogy of the Kings of Israel and Judah will help you better understand the lineage of the royal families in each nation. Using your preferred online browser, search "Genealogy of the Kings of Ancient Israel and Judah" for comparative genealogy or family trees. This can also help you see how the kings of Judah and Israel were sometimes related.

Maps: Cities, deserts, rivers—all these and more play a crucial role in what happened in Elisha's life. Search "Divided Kingdom" in Google Images or in a reproducible map book to find a map for that time period. A map will help you appreciate, for example, the distance covered by Elisha when he traveled to Damascus in Syria/Aram.

Lists: Browse "The Kings of Judah and Israel," and look for a comparative linear list of both kings. A list of these kings can help you know when the rulers of the two nations coincided with each other. Several kings had the same name, with some ruling at about the same time (Jehoram/Joram). For example, there were two Jeroboams (in Israel), two Ahaziahs (in Judah and Israel), two Jehorams, also known as Jorams (in Judah and Israel) and at least three Ben-Hadads! Could it be that baby books were scarce at that time to help parents select unique names?

Pictures and Photos: Pictures and photos can help you better understand the customs and geography of Elisha's day. You can find these in Bible bookstores and on the Internet. For example, a picture or drawing of an ancient iron axe can show how easy it would be for a blade to slip off its handle (2 Kings 6:5). A photo of ancient city wall ruins can illustrate how the king of Israel could be walking on the city wall (2 Kings 6:26).

Acting It Out: Instead of just reading the story, act it out! The stories of Elisha that contain conversations that lend themselves well for acting out portions of the stories. The narrator reads the non-conversation parts, and everyone else plays the parts of those speaking. Consider ones like the widow's oil (2 Kings 4:1-7), the "death in the pot" (2 Kings 4:38-40), and the healing of Naaman (2 Kings 5:8-27). To add some realism, use simple props (like a pot for the stew) and costumes (scarves for veils). Don't be afraid to be creative in your voice and body language to make the scenes come alive. Enjoy!

Archaeological artifacts: Archaeology can clarify your understanding of the Bible. Each future discovery has the possibility of enlightening your Bible study even further. Certain archaeological artifacts relate to Elisha's life and culture.

Check a Bible dictionary or encyclopedia to learn more about these:

- Lesson 1 — Ahab's ivory palace in Samaria (1 Kings 22:39; Amos 3:15, 6:4). Hundreds of pieces of ivory discovered in Samaria could be from panels and plaques covering walls and furniture in Ahab's palace.
- Lesson 4 — Mesha Stele/Mesha Inscription/Moabite Stone (2 Kings 3:4- 27). This Moabite king's version of the conflict with Israel includes a reference to Yahweh, the God of Israel,

and Chemosh, the god of Moab, as well as the tribe of Gad and Moabite towns mentioned in the Bible. The way this artifact was preserved from destruction is a fascinating story.

- Lesson 12 — Black Obelisk of Shalmaneser III (2 Kings 9-10). In this written and pictorial record, the obelisk shows King Jehu bowing on his knees to the Assyrian king. It is thought to be the only known surviving contemporary likeness of a king of Judah or Israel.

May God bless you as you study His Word!

ENDNOTES

Chapter 1 — Offering a Willing Heart
1. David Guzik and Robert Deffinbaugh, eds., *Layman's Bible Commentary, vol. 3: 1 Samuel thru 2 Kings*, (Uhrichsville, Ohio: Barbour, 2009), 147.
2. Iain W. Provan, *1 & 2 Kings* (Grand Rapids: Baker Books, 1995), 132.
3. Jeff Jenkins, "She Gave Away a Bible…and a Young Lady Learned about Jesus," June 9, 2010. The Good News: *http://www.oc.edu/good-news/story/she_gave_away_a_bible_._._._and_a_young_lady_learned_about_jesus* (June 7, 2018).

Chapter 2 — Following in Someone's Footsteps
1. Provan, *1 & 2 Kings*, 149.
2. Provan, *1 & 2 Kings*, 132.
3. John H. Walton, Victor H. Matthews, and Mark W. Chavalas, *The IVP Bible Background Commentary: Old Testament* (Downers Grove: InterVarsity Press, 2000), 377.
4. J. Hampton Keathley III, "Casting Shadows," *Studies in the Life of Elisha.* June 8, 2004. *Bible.org: https://bible.org/seriespage/casting-shadows* (June 8, 2018).
5. "Quotations about Jealousy." Quote Garden: *http://www.quotegarden.com/jealousy.html* (June 13, 2018).
6. "What We Do," *Orphan Care. Zambia Mission: https://www.zambiamission.org/orphancare* (June 30, 2018).
7. Jana Miller, "Hawley Spreading Hope and Love in Africa: Distinguished Young Alumna," *Vision: Oklahoma Christian University*, Fall 2013, *https://www.oc.edu/stories/content/hawley-spreading-hope-and-love-in-africa* (June 30, 2018).

Chapter 3 — Taking God Seriously
1. Walton, Matthews, and Chavalas, *The IVP Bible Background Commentary: Old Testament*, 376, 387.
2. Walter C. Kaiser Jr., Peter H. Davids, F. F. Bruce, and Manfred T. Brauch, *Hard Sayings of the Bible* (Downers Grove: InterVarsity Press, 1996), 232.
3. Donald Guthrie and Alec Motyer, eds., *The New Bible Commentary Revised* (Grand Rapids: Eerdmans, 1970), 350.
4. J. Hampton Keathley III, "Elisha and the Two Bears," *Studies in the Life of Elisha.* June 8, 2004. Bible.org: *https://bible.org/seriespage/elisha-and-two-bears-2-kings-223-25* (June 7, 2018).
5. Howard G. Hendricks and William D. Hendricks, *Living by the Book* (Chicago: Moody, 2007), 174-183.
6. "16 Glorious Quotes about the Promises of God," *Christian Quotes: https://www.christianquotes.info/top-quotes/16-glorious-quotes-promises-god/#axzz5HqIWq9oj* (June 8, 2018).
7. Cathy Meadows, letter to author, April 13, 2018.

Chapter 4 — Trusting When It Doesn't Make Sense
1. F.F. Bruce, *The International Bible Commentary*, rev ed. (Grand Rapids: Zondervan, 1986), 422.
2. Guthrie and Motyer, *The New Bible Commentary Revised*, 351.
3. Lynn McMillon, "On a Barnabas Journey of Service," December 21, 2016. *Christian Chronicle: https://christianchronicle.org/on-a-barnabus-journey-of-service/* (June 30, 2018).
4. McMillon, "On a Barnabas Journey."

Chapter 5 — Seeing the Importance of Little Things
1. 1. Arthur W. Klinck and Erich H. Kiehl. *Everyday Life in Bible Times, 3rd ed.* (St. Louis: Concordia, 1995), 58-59.
2. Rick Warren, "Servants Are Faithful in the Small Things," May 21, 2014. *Pastor Rick's Daily Hope: https://pastorrick.com/devotional/english/servants-are-faithful-in-the-small-things* (October 5, 2017).
3. Chellie Ison, "Wiggles, Fidgets and Buddies," April 6, 2017. *Christian Chronicle: https://christianchronicle.org/wiggles-fidgets-and-buddies/* (June 30, 2018).
4. Ison, "Wiggles, Fidgets and Buddies."

Chapter 6 — Cherishing Friendships
1. "Franklin Funnies," *Wit and Wisdom, 2002. Benjamin Franklin: http://www.pbs.org/benfranklin/l3_wit_franklin.html* (June 12, 2018).
2. Klinck and Kiehl, *Everyday Life,* 164.
3. Walton, Matthews, and Chavalas, *The IVP Bible Background Commentary: Old Testament,* 389.
4. Kayla Barker, email message to author, April 26, 2018.

Chapter 7 — Feasting in a Family
1. Guthrie and Motyer, *The New Bible Commentary Revised,* 351.
2. Walton, Matthews, and Chavalas, *The IVP Bible Background Commentary: Old Testament,* 390.
3. Guzik and Deffinbaugh, *Layman's Bible Commentary,* vol. 3, 180.
4. American Psychological Association, "Social isolation, loneliness could be greater threat to public health than obesity," August 5, 2017. *ScienceDaily: https://www.sciencedaily.com/releases/2017/08/170805165319.htm* (June 16, 2018).
5. "C. S. Lewis," *AZ Quotes: http://www.azquotes.com/quote/458116* (July 16, 2018).
6. "Helping Hands for Christ Ladies Outreach," *Cleveland Church of Christ: https://clevelandcofc.com/helping-hands/* (June 29, 2018).
7. Douglas Dingley, email message to author, May 9, 2018.

Chapter 8 — Embracing Humility
1. David Roper, *Seasoned with Salt: Lessons from Elisha* (Grand Rapids: Discovery House, 2004), 85.
2. Walton, Matthews, and Chavalas, *The IVP Bible Background Commentary: Old Testament,* 391.
3. "Quotations about Humility," October 18, 2017. *The Quote Garden: www.quotegarden.com/humility.html* (June 19, 2018).
4. Ibid.
5. Ibid.
6. Ibid.
7. Beth Wilson, email message to author, August 8, 2018.

Chapter 9 — Opening Your Eyes
1. Bob Deffinbaugh, "The Life and Times of Elisha the Prophet - Saved from the Syrians: The War that Never Happened (2 Kings 6:1-23)," *Profiting from the Prophets.* August 24, 2004. *Bible.org: https://bible.org/seriespage/life-and-times-elisha-prophet%E2%80%94-saved-syrians-war-never-happened-2-kings-61-23* (June 21, 2018).
2. Kaiser Jr., Davids, Bruce, and Brauch, *Hard Sayings of the Bible,* 235.
3. Clinton E. Arnold, ed., *Zondervan Illustrated Bible Backgrounds Commentary: vol. 3, Romans to Philemon* (Grand Rapids: Zondervan, 2002), 309-310.
4. Rachel Pate, "Laurie Novak: Saying Yes to God's Dreams," *Christian Woman* (May/June 2014), 12-15.

5. Pate, "Laurie Novak," 15.
6. Ibid.

Chapter 10 — Reporting Good News
1. Anne Murray. "A Little Good News." YouTube Video, 2.34. Posted by "happysun," June 17, 2014. *Anne Murray: A Little Good News (2003): https://www.youtube.com/watch?v=BOR6Vx-Ogbk* (June 22, 2018).
2. Walton, Matthews, and Chavalas, *The IVP Bible Background Commentary: Old Testament,* 393-394.
3. Stafford North, *Evangelizing Your Community* (Nashville: 21st Century Christian, 2007).
4. North, *Evangelizing Your Community,* 107.
5. Bailey McBride, "Jo Anne North's Devotion Yields a Bountiful Harvest Behind Bars," February 25, 2015. *Christian Chronicle: https://christianchronicle.org/joanne-north-s-devotion-yields-a-bountiful-harvest-behind-bars/* (June 29, 2018).
6. Stafford North, "Letters from Prison," January 7, 2014. *The Good News: http://www.oc.edu/good-news/story/letters_from_prison* (June 29, 2018).

Chapter 11 — Weeping When Others Weep
1. Provan, *1 & 2 Kings,* 207.
2. Trent C. Butler, ed., "Hazael," *Holman Bible Dictionary. 1991. Studylight.org: https://www.studylight.org/dictionaries/hbd/h/hazael.html* (June 23, 2018).
3. "Weeping Quotes," *AZ Quotes: http://www.azquotes.com/quotes/topics/weeping.html* (June 22, 2018).
4. Jane McWhorter, *Special Delivery: A Course in Letter Writing* (Huntsville: Publishing Designs, 2004), 179.
5. Jenny Duncan, letter to author, September 5, 2018.

Chapter 12 — Checking Your Motives
1. Walton, Matthews, and Chavalas, *The IVP Bible Background Commentary: Old Testament,* 398-399, 752.
2. Elizabeth Achtemeier, *Minor Prophets 1* (Peabody, Mass.: Hendrickson, 1996), 16.
3. Gleason L. Archer. *Encyclopedia of Bible Difficulties* (Grand Rapids: Regency Reference Library, 1982), 207-209.
4. Stafford North, "Small Oklahoma Church Succeeds with After-School Program," November 9, 2015. *The Good News: http://www.oc.edu/good-news/story/small-oklahoma-church-succeeds-with-after-school-program* (June 29, 2018).
5. Andy Hutchinson, email message to author, April 4, 2018.

Chapter 13 — Leaving a Lasting Legacy
1. Trent C. Butler, ed., "Elisha," *Holman Bible Dictionary. 1991. Studylight.org: https://www.studylight.org/dictionaries/hbd/e/elisha.html* (June 26, 2018).
2. Provan, *1 and 2 Kings,* 228.
3. Bruce, *The International Bible Commentary,* 430.
4. Provan, *1 and 2 Kings,* 233-234.
5. Erik Tryggestad, "Haiti: Finding Hope in a Broken Place," April 1, 2010. *Christian Chronicle: https://christianchronicle.org/haiti-finding-hope-in-a-broken-place/* (June 30, 2018).
6. Nancy Coats Posey and others, "A Tribute to Roberta Edwards," *Christian Woman* (January/February 2016), 11.
7. Erik Tryggestad, "Christians Honor Slain Missionary," November 21, 2015. *Christian Chronicle: https://christianchronicle.org/christians-honor-slain-missionary/* (June 30, 2018).
8. Rita Cochrane and others, "A Tribute to Roberta Edwards," *Christian Woman* (January/February 2016), 11.

Printed in the USA
CPSIA information can be obtained
at www.ICGtesting.com
JSHW010228310723
45566JS00003B/13